FROM FEAR TO LOVE

Books by Harry Willson

nonfiction
From Fear To Love: My Journey Beyond Christianity
Myth and Mortality: Testing the Stories
Freedom From God: Restoring the Sense of Wonder

fiction
Johnny Plutonium, and Other Survival Stories
This'll Kill Ya, and Other Dangerous Stories
Duke City Tales: Stories from Albuquerque
Souls and Cells Remember: A Love Story
A World For the Meek: A Fantasy Novel

FROM FEAR TO LOVE

My Journey Beyond Christianity

Harry Willson

edited by Zelda Leah Gatuskin

AMADOR PUBLISHERS, LLC

Copyright© 2012 by Harry Willson

Edited by Zelda Leah Gatuskin

All rights reserved, including the right to reproduce this book or any part thereof, in any form, except for inclusion of brief quotes for a review.

Printed in the United States of America
First Printing, 2012
Second Printing, 2021
ISBN: 978-0-938513-42-1
Library of Congress Control Number: 2012939445

AMADOR PUBLISHERS, LLC
Albuquerque, New Mexico USA
www.amadorbooks.com

EDITOR'S NOTE

Harry Willson's "philosophical memoir" was written in the mid-1990s. Not only has Harry pinned it down here by stating his age at the start as 62, but he spoke about his "enquiry" often during those years. As far as I can tell, the work proceeded apace with *Freedom From God* and *Myth and Mortality* (2002 and 2007 respectively, Amador Publishers). When this, his exploration of direct life experience, required additional study, or articulation of an overarching history and philosophy, Harry poured those efforts into the other two volumes to produce a trio of books he came to refer to as his "humanist trilogy."

I found this first-last of the manuscripts in rather good shape, but it was clear that Harry had lifted elements from it to develop in more detail in the other books, and tweaked the original work as he did so. He certainly planned to go over *From Fear To Love* again before publishing. He would have invited and accepted editorial input from a few trusted others, including myself, so I have proceeded in our usual fashion through the process he taught me, with the only difference being that now I get to have the final say instead of him.

Well, sort of. After several rounds of editing, I found myself un-editing. Questions to do with punctuation, the styling of words (god, God and "God," for instance) and invented word forms (ecclesiasticating, creedal, extincted), all suddenly felt resolved. I got it. I got what he was saying, why and how he was saying it, at the time he was writing. It is subtle in some cases, but the man was a theologian, mythologist, teacher, linguist, writer and publisher, as well as a dynamic public speaker—he knew how to get his point across. He preferred to present a folksy rather than academic impression, but he was well versed in all the "rules" of language and writing. In the last round of editing, I referred all outstanding questions back to that version of the manuscript I found on Harry's computer, and put myself in mind of the many editorial sessions we'd shared. "Leave it," Harry would command when someone was getting too fussy or intrusive. And when the edits made it better, he'd approve with a hearty, "*¡Formidable!*"

Zelda Leah Gatuskin, 2012

dedicated to Adela Amador Willson
June 1922 – May 2012

FROM FEAR TO LOVE
Contents

PART I. HOW GOD DIED
1. A Crutch Lost 3
2. What to Believe 5
3. Daisy Chain of Theologies 8
4. Myth 11
5. Dream 12
6. That Voice 15
7. The Beloved Community 20
8. How It Began 22
9. Fundamentalism 26
10. The Bible 37
11. Saved by the Glands 45
12. Church History 48
13. The Original Lie 52
14. Boring from Within 56
15. Caretaker Religion 62
16. Heretic 65
17. Social Action 73
18. Demission 81

PART II. PROPHET WITH NO GOD
19. The Office 87
20. Residue 97
21. Teacher 100
22. Language 108
23. Science and Nature 114
24. Social Protest 122
25. God, and Angels 132
26. Human Nature 153
27. Success and Prosperity 158

PART III. BIG QUESTIONS REMAIN
28. Memory 167
29. Health Care 172
30. Mortality 176
31. Reincarnation 186
32. Openness 193
33. Misanthropy 202
34. Ego and Self 209
35. Conclusion 217

PART IV. AFTERWORDS
36. Editor's Interlude 221
37. Care 224
38. Thoughts While Playing the Piano 225

ABOUT
Harry Willson 227
Zelda Leah Gatuskin 229

PART I

◆

HOW GOD DIED

1. A CRUTCH LOST

Why this hesitation, this difficulty putting down the first word—the inclination, stopped in mid-air, was to write, "I"— I'm doing the thinking, the remembering, the writing. Didn't I make the decision to undertake this examination? Isn't it my life that is to be exposed here?

Not really, perhaps. Not entirely *my* life—it's not something one possesses. It was not my decision, exactly, either, this writing, which is now begun, ready or not.

I shall have to use the word "I" in order to do this. It's false modesty, and annoying delay, to pretend otherwise. Circumlocutions have their place, I firmly believe—I'm convinced we should insert long and cumbersome ones wherever others so glibly insert "God," for instance—but I'm not going to take the trouble to circumlocute "I." Not at this stage of the examination, anyway.

I recently passed my sixtieth birthday. I began using the phrase, "Second Half Journey," ten years ago, when I was fifty. I gathered a file of observations with that label. Think of life as a circle, a large flat wheel. You ride along on the wheel. As you ride you can look across and see, dimly, the other side of the wheel. When you're twenty, you can look across and see forty—sometime in your future. When you're forty, you can look across and see eighty, and you'll go ahead and assume that that's in your future. I did, anyway. When you're fifty, you're not so sure. My great-grandmother lived to be 101. My father died of emphysema at age 89, and he and all of us believed he could have reached 100 if he hadn't smoked for seventy-five years.

Now past sixty, I look across that wheel of life, which turns faster than it used to, and the other side is a point in the past, not the future. It happened when I wasn't looking. I got into the second half.

When I passed fifty, I was aware that I had lost a crutch that I'd been carrying since childhood. I had found it in the Bible— I learned that book when I was very young. I fully mastered the content of the stories before I was twenty. Then I learned the original languages, Greek and Hebrew, before I was twenty-five. One way or another, the Bible has been an important element in this life that is now going to be examined.

Anyway, when the Pharisees and the Sadducees were cross-examining Jesus, he kept referring to God as his father, and kept implying that he wasn't going to die.

"Are you greater than our father Abraham?" they asked. "*He* died!"

"Your father Abraham rejoiced that he was to see my day," Jesus said, and one may wonder what he meant by that. "He saw it and was glad," Jesus added.

"You are not yet fifty years old," they said, "and have you seen Abraham?"

Then comes the famous answer, which makes this little section memorable to most readers and critics. Jesus said to them, "Before Abraham was, I am."

Well, my little crutch, which I used for decades, was that earlier phrase, "You are not yet fifty years old..." I used it to justify failure, procrastination, and a thing I then called laziness but now no longer do, since I have come to regard the impulse to-never-rest, which I had, as a form of serious mental illness. I used my little crutch, saying to myself, justifying myself, getting myself back into motion, "You are not yet fifty years old, Harry. You still have time. The clock is ticking, however. Get going. Get at it."

Then one day, more than ten years ago, it was no longer true. I could no longer say to myself, "You are not yet fifty years old." Gone was that crutch, that excuse, that whip. Now, at last, it feels like good riddance.

2. WHAT TO BELIEVE

At sixty, I'm enjoying very much this stage of my life. Far more than childhood, which is supposed to be so carefree and peaceful, and in my case wasn't. Far, far more than adolescence, which was no fun at all. I like being one of the elders; I like the slower pace. I don't feel that the pace is being forced on me by a deteriorating physical condition. Instead it feels like I'm smartening up a little. I don't need to push so hard. My effort is not what turns the great Wheel of Being. Good things happen without my effort, almost in spite of all my contriving. All the wasted effort—for a while I thought that's what it was, but I feel that less now. Maybe I'm accepting the fact that all that fruitless, thankless work helped make me what I now am, and since I'm beginning to accept and like the person that I am, all that effort wasn't wasted or bad. But I push less now.

I used to resent the notion that what was happening to me, what I was going through, was preparation for something that was pending. "Well, when am I finally ready? I feel ready! Why not now? If not now, when? Why is it always delayed, while I prepare more?" The good things I thought I wanted then aren't so important now. A larger income. Payment for work done. Some recognition. What I have now, and what I am now, is very fine—and I've translated the old it's-all-just-preparation notion into the writer's comment, no matter what he's experiencing: "It's all copy." If nothing else, I'll make a story out of each adventure. The people I feel sorry for are those with no adventures. I feel sorry, but I stay away from them. Don't tell me you're bored!

This enquiry will be full of stories. Incidents I remember. Wisdom that I've been exposed to, and am now at last old enough to appreciate. Insights I've come to by examining my life. "The unexamined life is not worth living." Socrates said that. It's *not* in the Bible, and most church activity discourages self-examination, really, but I subscribed to the examined-life idea somehow, early on, and still do.

I am not going to recount everything that happened to me. I mean I'm not even going to try. I did spend one year, fifteen years ago, trying to remember and record every pre-teenage memory I could dredge up. It did me good.

But this examination has a theme—and here again I find myself hesitating—sorting words, weighing one against another—what *is* this theme? Faith, maybe. Myth and Truth, maybe. Are they in conflict? Most think so. I do not think so.

My wife, Adela, and I were discussing our disappointment in the behavior of a certain person after a recent public confrontation. "I thought he'd speak up," I said. "I can't believe he didn't say anything."

"It's no surprise," she stated. *"No tiene credo."* Adela uses both languages, all the time. The wishy-washy, undependable behavior could be accounted for, she thought, by noting, *"No tiene credo."* It could be translated, "He has no creed," but it's not exactly a creed, like the Apostles' Creed or the Nicene Creed. It doesn't necessarily mean a historical official belief system. It could almost be translated, "He doesn't believe in anything." Or even better, "He doesn't know what he believes." His undependable behavior, which triggered this discussion, is due to the fact that he lacks a well-thought-out set of convictions.

This enquiry has to do with that, as it pertains to me. I was born into one of those old official belief systems, The Presbyterian Church, and bought into it as a child. I then spent decades working myself, and thinking myself, out of it, or on past it, as I would now say. I am a post-Christian, not an ex-Christian. For a while I was really "out of it," and resentful of the time and effort wasted. More than three decades! Half a life! But I have come to believe that one cannot be faulted for starting where one did, and that liberation, at any age, is better than continued bondage. "The only thing that we done wrong was stayin' in the wilderness too long! Keep your eye on the prize!"

I have observed that some, when they get to this stage on the Path of Liberation, look back and dismiss all of that which they needed liberation *from* as crap, nonsense and worse than nonsense. I felt that for a while, but now do not. I find myself living, as never before, "by faith." I find the sense of wonder alive and well within me. I find myself more submissive to—to what? Words fail me. I choke and gag on the word "God," as we shall see. But there's something—not an Entity, even—maybe simply The Whole Thing—what is It up to?

I do not believe that existence is meaningless. I see order and purpose everywhere, except in the behavior of organized human groups. In atoms, in galaxies, inside myself, in those beautiful people with whom I share life and thoughts like these—I see something. Not that I've come back, like a Prodigal Son, to Authority. I have not done that, and cannot foresee doing it. But I've been made aware, like I never was when I was a faithful, loyal, official, professional holy man. What is this?

I asked several of those closest to me, "Do you regard me as a man of faith?" At first they stalled. The phrase sounded churchy, and they knew I didn't have any contact with organized religion anymore. Their stalling made me stall, too. Could it be said of me, *"No tiene credo"*? No one I have asked thinks so. So then, Harry, if you don't believe *that*, that old system, but you do believe something, what is it that you do believe? That's the theme of this enquiry. And related to it is this question, "How does what you believe affect what you do?" Not what you say, or even what you write (writing is a form of saying, and one can lie…), but what you *do*!

3. A DAISY CHAIN OF THEOLOGIES

My life, and this enquiry, have to do with myth, from Parsifal to Faust, from Trickster Coyote to Indira's necklace. I find myself in all of them.

As a boy I loved the Norse myths, and then the Greek. I learned the Bible stories as Truth, and became alarmed when it was first suggested that they, too, were myths. The fact that I was able to accept the fact that Christianity *was* myth during my college studies, before I ever went to seminary, meant that I stayed with it longer than I would have otherwise. I could have rejected Christianity, from a rationalist scientific point of view, as simply false, and never learned the Greek and Hebrew and all that horrible, horrifying church history. At this point I'm glad that I did not reject it then, too early and too easily.

Instead I went all the way through it. At the time I was born, my parents were serious church-going people, caught up in the Oxford Movement of the early 1930s. My father was from English Quaker and German Pietist stock in Pennsylvania. My mother had come from Scotland and the Presbyterian Church. I came into awareness taking quite for granted a conservative sort of Protestant Christianity. Fundamentalism was around, in Bible Tabernacle summer episodes and some summer church camp counselors. I flirted seriously with a fundamentalist group, called Intervarsity Christian Fellowship, during one year in college. I separated from them with the conclusion that they were really mean-hearted, cruel and unpleasant people, who ballyhooed a god that I found to be unjust and immoral and unkind. In seminary I learned the history of the fundamentalist movement, and my study of the original languages made the fundamentalist teaching of the inerrancy of Scripture totally ridiculous. The only reason I think fundamentalism is worth bothering to refute is that they have grabbed political power in many places, and are therefore dangerous as well as ridiculous.

In seminary we studied what the fundies called Barthianism, after Karl Barth. It was also called Neo-orthodoxy. It feels extremely conservative to me, now, but was hopelessly way-out and "liberal" from the fundamentalist point of view. In classes we studied Emil Bruner's books even more than Karl Barth's. God was sovereign, utterly. Kierkegaard and Bonhoeffer illustrated "radical obedience." I tried to illustrate it, too, in my life, and became a Spanish-speaking Presbyterian missionary in New Mexico.

I kept reading and thinking, and I noticed that some of my colleagues did not. Others of us met in small informal groups and conferences. I became involved in the local community and found myself championing "liberal" causes in the name of the gospel I was preaching.

I opposed the bomb-shelter craze of the early '60s, convinced that it was a way of sanctioning nuclear war. No Christian would build a bomb shelter and then defend it and its contents with a rifle. He would give all he had to feed the poor and then die—and meanwhile he would preach and protest and scream that nuclear war was an evil abomination, totally unapproved by God and the Prince of Peace. This was the message I kept proclaiming—in a town that made its living from a nuclear weapons laboratory.

I found myself caught up in the Black Liberation Movement. I came to believe that Martin Luther King was the last best hope for humanity and for Christianity. Nonviolent insistence on justice for all could head off the pending revolution—if it didn't, Christianity was going to be irrelevant, I thought. I watched the churches reject

Martin Luther King and his cause, until after he was murdered; then they helped build and adorn the tomb and monuments of one more dead prophet, per usual. And I observed that standard-brand Protestant churches became more and more irrelevant to daily life in this world.

I opposed the Vietnam War from the very first, since the days of Eisenhower and John Foster Dulles. Most Presbyterians were proud that Dulles was a fellow church member, but I was not. My opposition to the war led me into more and more activism: protests, marches, sit-ins, teach-ins—I became known in town as the radical, hippie, Commie, even black (although I'm not an African American), angry young preacher.

Meanwhile I was reading and thinking, and finding myself not believing more and more of what I was supposed to be teaching. "Americans had better be hoping that there is *not* a just God," I thought. "What will happen to Albuquerque if peace breaks out?"

I attended a summer session at the Presbyterian Seminary in San Francisco. Thoughts I had been feeling guilty about thinking were pronounced aloud from the lectern. The relation of early Christianity to myth was spelled out, and parallel stories carefully read and compared. I was left with a kind of homemade gospel of human solidarity, but not much of a God. The doctrine of God became the crucial question for me. The doctrine of the church had never amounted to much in my thinking, and was long gone. I lasted only one more year, pretending one could continue to "bore from within." I found out that I, at least, could not.

I found myself outside the institution—starved out by a non-supportive congregation. That part was hardly any wonder. I was sliding through the history of Protestant theology, and exposing it to the people, or them to it. I noticed again that most pastors did not do that. Neo-conservative, liberal, social gospel, de-mythologization, re-mythologization—it was all too much, too fast. Parishioners complained, very candidly, "We don't want to hear about the prophets and their message for our time. We want comfort!" That particular statement came from a woman whose son was at that very time giving himself cancer by dumping Agent Orange on the rain forests and the peoples of Vietnam. What comfort could I give?

It was hopeless. I had found the God-is-dead theology during that summer in San Francisco. I preached it, lectured about it, including on local TV, and became known as the local God-is-dead theologian. Actually, the more famous God-is-dead theologians (Altizer, Hamilton, Vahanian) puzzled me. I took the key phrase to mean, "What we thought was God, isn't. What we were worshipping is an idol made by us. *That* God is dead." But those guys seemed to be saying, and meaning literally somehow, that the sovereign God who made heaven and earth and ruled all things had put in and died and that we should have a funeral. I was as puzzled as anybody, really, but one phrase from Hamilton was not puzzling: "The faith is flawed, but the love is not." I coasted for a little while on love, and then found myself outside, and more alone than I had ever been.

4. MYTH

When the local congregational support failed, I did not move to another parish, which is what usually happens when the situation deteriorates to the "starve-him-out" stage. Instead, I left the organized church entirely.

The cosmos provided a job teaching school in a private boys' academy. The sixth grade boys and I together stumbled on the world of myth. All the legends and fairy tales and myths of all the world—we gobbled them up. I discovered Joseph Campbell, decades before Bill Moyers put him on TV, and I read everything he wrote. We exchanged letters after I finished his four-volume *Masks Of God*. I thanked him for saving my life.

I had spent several years as a zombie, thinking I had invested my entire adult intellectual enterprise on what I had come to believe was baloney. The myths of the world, and Campbell's presentation of what he calls the "monomyth," helped me get it all back into perspective. Christianity is not *the* Way. When it claims to be, it is simply in error, and is offensive. But it can be, for some, *a* way. It was not the height of useless stupidity on my part to understand it fully, including its history and its "sacred" texts. I began to recover.

I fell into a study of the Tarot, and came to see it as another version of that same single unifying monomyth. The same story, the same hero's journey, the minority report buried under the bloody rubble and splendor of Western Christian Civilization—the Tarot is our western version of yoga and of Zen and of the Tao. I taught Campbell's *Hero With A Thousand Faces* to the seniors at that same academy, and I learned more thereby than they did.

So myth has been and remains important in my life. I do not have a group, except the group of two, which is this marriage, and a few special friends with whom we share this heavy, deep, weird stuff.

5. DREAM

We get at myth, or let's say we *experience* myth directly, by paying attention to our dreams. I borrowed a chapter title from Campbell's *Hero*, and taught a course at the academy called "Myth and Dream." We studied the writing of dream analysts like Freud, Fromm, Jung, and Perls. Mostly we brought our dreams to class and shared them and tried to understand them.

After leaving teaching, I continued facilitating dream workshops. We agreed to meet for eight evenings, once a week, to share our dreams and our intuitive responses to each other's dreams. We found ourselves dreaming "classic" dreams with classic archetypal themes. Some remarkable things happened to the participants, especially to me.

"The dream is the private myth. The myth is the public dream." That is from Joseph Campbell's *The Power Of Myth*. We all find ourselves in archetypal human situations throughout our lives: the Fork in the Road, Helpers, Hinderers, Labors, Distant Goals, the Quest, the Father, the Mother, the Path. All of that is inside each one of us.

My earliest dream that I still remember was very, very early. I may have been three years old, or even younger. I am alone in my room, in my bed. It is an Audience, not a Vision. The dream consists of a deep, resonating, accusing Voice, calling my name twice: "Harry! Harry!" When I tell this, I cup my hands and lower the pitch and emphasize both syllables, to imitate that dread Voice. "Harry! Harry!"

I am terrified. I answer, "What?" But there is no more message. Just the Voice, calling my name, summoning me, accusing me, but not telling me *what*.

Early on, I assumed it was God. God was taken quite for granted in that household. I was taken to church in a basket when only weeks old, and the little church was part of my earliest consciousness. The Bible stories were my early childhood nursery stories. I learned to read from the book, *First Steps For Little Feet*, which retold Bible stories with accompanying ugly line drawings, and had questions at the end of each story. I became very good at answering the questions, and I learned the stories.

By the age of ten, I was reading the Bible itself in the old King James translation. The Gospels, with Jesus' words in red ink, the Book of Acts, and narrative parts of the Old Testament became familiar to me early on. The prophets and epistles remained too obscure to follow until the new translation, the RSV (Revised Standard Version), came out while I was in high school.

I found stories that paralleled my dream—that Audience where

I heard my name repeated. Jesus said to Simon Peter, "Simon, Simon." The resurrected Jesus said to Saul on the road to Damascus, "Saul, Saul."

The best one is in the Old Testament. Samuel has been given to the old High Priest, Eli, as an apprentice. He has his own little room in the Temple. One night he hears a Voice calling, "Samuel! Samuel!" Aha! The same Audience, the same Voice.

Samuel runs to Eli. "Here I am, for you called me."

"No, I didn't call you. Go lie down again."

Samuel goes to his room and lies down. Again he hears the Voice, "Samuel! Samuel!"

Samuel runs to Eli again, "Here I am, for you called me."

"No, I didn't call you. Go, lie down again," Eli says.

When it happens a third time, Eli comprehends that God is calling Samuel, and tells him, "God is calling you. When he calls again, answer him with these words, 'Speak, Lord, for thy servant heareth.'"

Samuel goes and lies down. The Voice calls again, "Samuel! Samuel!"

Samuel answers, "Speak, Lord, for thy servant heareth."

And then the story changes. It becomes a tirade in which God is giving royal hell to Eli about how he was not restraining his evil sons, on and on, and how God will take the office of High Priest away from Eli's family—all that political stuff, one could say—all surely of very little interest to a young boy seeking answers.

The Voice, even in Samuel's story, doesn't really tell Samuel what to do. It leaves Samuel dangling, and it left me dangling.

I tried Samuel's answer. "Speak, Lord, for thy servant heareth." I never received any additional information, much as I wanted it. Throughout the rest of my childhood and youth, I found myself looking for concrete answers to the question, "What does God want of me—what does God want me to do?" God never ever really said, in that Voice of his. All he did with *that* was call my name, frightening me, and setting in motion a readiness *not* to be in charge of my own life.

6. THAT VOICE

The youth group at church had as its expressed purpose: "To discover God's will for our lives, and do it." Do it. Something to go do. But what? For lack of any more information from the Voice, I had to make up answers. I put answers in God's mouth and then relieved the pressure I felt to obey, by going and doing *those* things.

What does God want a young boy to do? The search for the answer kept me out of trouble, that is, the overt obvious trouble that so many kids nowadays get into. Sex, drugs, crime—this search for God's will made all that unthinkable, literally unimaginable. I suppose I should be grateful for the protection.

But that same search poisoned much of the spontaneity of youth. I was far too serious. I found the phrase for it years later in the movie, *A Thousand Clowns*. I was a "middle-aged kid." I know more now about pleasure, relaxation and spontaneous fun as a middle-aged, that is, *older* middle-aged man, than I ever did as a kid.

The Voice was a torment. I did try to obey it, which wasn't easy, since the Voice refused to be specific. Still, I let it govern what I was trying to do with my life, and when I finally quit doing that, I was full of resentment at all the time and energy I'd wasted.

That Voice, and my attempt to obey it, gave my life a direction, a structure, a sense of purpose, which seems rare in many other lives, especially young ones. "I'll go to medical school, even though I don't like the prospect much, because God wants me to." "I'll survive on thirty bucks a week, with wife and family, because God wants me to." "I'll go to a place I've never seen and serve as a missionary to people I've never met, because God wants me to." That kind of resolve enabled me to do things that seem either stupid or impossible or both from any practical perspective, but at least it was not drifting, not careening toward disaster, which seems to describe so many lives I observe. Again, maybe I should be more grateful to that Voice, that illusion, than I have so far allowed myself to be.

I do not now believe that the Voice was God. I do not believe that God is an entity "out there," who can call and terrify a child. I suppose the Voice was what Freud called the super-ego, some kind of internalization of the authority of my father. An important clue is that when I figured out "God" and left organized Christianity, I found myself feuding, mostly by mail, with my father. And I did not find complete peace until he died, ten days after his final failed attempt to force me to obey, dictated from his death-bed, when I was 53 and he was 88. He reared up in his bed, more alert than I had seen him during that entire final visit, pointed a finger at me and declared, "I want you to move back to Pennsylvania, soon, and permanently!" emphasizing the adverbs with jabs of the pointing finger.

I laughed it off, saying that I had my life and it was out there in New Mexico. He allowed no more conversation. "Goodbye, then," he said, and repeated it, when attempts were tried to renew the languishing conversation around his bed. "Goodbye, then." And it *was* goodbye.

The Voice is silent now, at last. I hear echoes, sometimes, especially in bed awake at night, but I call that "residue," and attribute it to habit. The Voice is silent and the echoes grow ever fainter, thank the Powers That Be.

Language is tricky. *What* Powers That Be? I do not mean political powers downtown or in Washington, DC. I mean *what* in place of "God"? If there is no Entity that made everything, and rules it and torments it, what is there? It has become the basic question, and includes these also: "Why write this stuff?" "Why tell all this?"

Bertrand Russell wrote *Why I Am Not A Christian* to clarify for himself and others what kept him out of that institution. He was probably hoping to lure some of his readers out, or keep them out if they were already out. I'm not deliberately addressing this to Christians, professional or other, nor to non-Christians or anti-Christians. I guess my enquiry is essentially private. It's for me. I need to know what I believe—I, a man who *sí, tiene credo*.

If I believed that there simply is no "God"—if I were convinced that "God" was just a lie invented by priests long ago so that they could grab power over people—I could rejoice and relax in my unbelief and spare myself this endeavor. I have come to believe that "God" is a metaphor, which indeed has been grabbed and taken over by priests and priestly types to place at the heart of their racket. But part of the reason that racket has been so successful over the eons is that the original metaphor had an element of Truth and Power in it. The word "God," which I don't use anymore because it's so contaminated with error and worse things, nevertheless corresponds, or once did correspond, to something —as a metaphor.

There is more to life than meets the eye. Logical positivism says, "Nothing is mysterious! Away with the sense of wonder!" Materialism says, "Physical matter is all there is!" But they are philosophical blind alleys that do not correspond with what up-to-date empirical science is discovering, let alone with what we know by intuition about ourselves and each other.

Some of my best friends believe in angels. I'm dubious, I'll admit, because of my logical training and my limited experience. True, *"angelos"* means "messenger," and I have had some strange experiences with unexpected messengers. I think of a certain parakeet in particular, and a mockingbird. But "messengers"? From where? From whom?

"Oh, Love, That Will Not Let Me Go"—it was one of my favorite hymns from my church days. I can make it make a kind of sense, even yet, although I refuse to let "Oh, Love" equal "Oh, God," or "Oh, Christ." There is an underlying love, an overarching love—and I even sense, still, that it will not let *me* go—but what *is* this? What?

In my study of myth, which was accompanied by studies of cosmology and consciousness, I finally concluded that the sense of wonder was a good thing, and ought not to be allowed to atrophy in this age of unified theories and easy answers. "The Best Questions Don't Have Answers" was a poster on my wall all the years I taught school.

Natural phenomena can be great aids to devotion. A summer evening with several million fireflies. The aurora borealis on a winter night with the temperature near zero. The first glimpse of the ocean after being away for months, or years. The stillness in the scorching desert. Any non-urban glimpse of the Milky Way. The contents of a drop of pond water, seen through a microscope. The sense of open space and mystery, as one stares into the face of a friend. An analysis of the unlikely chain of events that led to this personal moment, amid all that confusion!

I have decided that "God" can be a metaphor for What There Is. I doubt that the metaphor was arrived at that way originally. I mean, I suspect that Early Man personified everything, and the fact that everything had a spirit led to separating the spirit from the thing itself, say, the Wind and the Spirit of the Wind. "Spirit" means "wind"! The Volcano and the Spirit of the Volcano. Then all the spirits were arranged in hierarchies and companies, as early theologians got to work. The invention of the King, the State, the Emperor, and War itself, led to spirits, or gods, that governed those things, or represented those things. The "God" who died at the hands of Nietzsche and the God-is-dead theologians of the 1960s was one of those war gods—a god of Authority and Power and

How God Died 19

Vengeance and Justice and Mercy. A potentate of ancient and modern times. So, *he* died, and I'm thankful. To whom am I thankful?

Perhaps my notion that "God" can be a metaphor for The Whole Thing can only be arrived at the way I arrived at it. If you never believed in God, and never tried to obey God, you're unimpressed by this marvelous breakthrough. I have, as a matter of fact, never found anyone as excited about this as I am. It's like discovering the cure to a disease that nobody else has.

Well, I had it, and I'm going to proceed. "God" can be a metaphor for What There Is, All of It, As It Is, Doing What It Does, inexorable in its execution of Whatever Comes Next, just in its insistence that every action has an equal and opposite reaction, totally interconnected with itself with no parts left out, all One. I didn't make this up. This is Monism, the heart of magic and occult teaching. "Each is both." "That which is above is as that which is below." "There is One."

Let's look at some of the "isms."

Theism—there is God.

Atheism—there is no god.

Pantheism—everything is God.

Polytheism—there are many gods.

Monotheism—the great breakthrough, supposedly, that there is only one God.

Monism—There is One. There is only one thing. Everything is all one, only one. I don't want to call it "God," so I'm no good as a pantheist or a monotheist. Yet I don't call myself an atheist, either, because an atheist, maybe, is one of those who *no tiene credo,* who doesn't believe anything, and I guess that's not me.

I do think that monotheism, especially Christianity, teaches much nonsense, especially as it inflates individual human egos. Many monotheists think that God is stupid—racists, for example. If there's only one God, how can he belong to some and not others?

They reduce the supposed source of Truth and Justice and Power and Meaning in all the Cosmos to some little secret weapon they can keep in their pockets and then pull out when they're up to fresh meanness.

Monism is better. I am part of It. It is doing Its thing, temporarily and partly, through me. But I shy away from dividing all of existence into two parts, the Me and the not-Me. Those two parts are too disparate in age, size, power and "importance." It's less ego-inflating and less of a burden to transfer my sense of loyalty and my devotion away from me, my little ego, to It. Then I can laugh and relax, because It is irresistible, all-powerful, safe and secure. The Whole Thing is all right.

Francis Thompson wrote a powerful poem, "The Hound of Heaven," which used to remind me of that Voice— "I fled him, down the nights and down the days. I fled him down the arches of the years…"

The personification, "him," grates a little, but the sense that It, which I am still ready to call "Love," will not let me go, persists.

7. THE BELOVED COMMUNITY

In the name of farming and soil conservation, Wendell Berry writes of "The Beloved Community." It was a phrase used in the churches in my missionary days in the 1960s. It's a bad button for me, so bad that I still have a horrible time with group meetings, and cannot force myself to join any kind of group. Berry uses "Beloved Community" in two ways, to refer to "the natural neighborhood" and to "the contrived group." I have experienced both things, and both experiences were bad.

The natural neighborhood was Montoursville, Pennsylvania, in the 1930s and 40s. I was born there and lived there until I went to college in 1949, but I was always an outsider. It was a town which took pride in the fact that there were "no Jews, no Catholics and no niggers." The native Susquehannocks had been exterminated. My father came from the rural boondocks up the creek, and my mother came from Scotland. Her accent labeled her a foreigner. I have come to suspect that my sense of kinship with "black" and "red" people is based on the fact that I, too, was excluded from the place where I was born, put out at the start and kept out, never let in. My way of making it bearable was to convert being "put out" into being "sent out." Mission! Missionary! Whenever I went back it was never satisfactory, except as a way and a place to clarify memory, to put away more and more childish things, to let more and more truth out, painful as that always was. Now that my parents are dead I do not go back at all. The notion of being accepted into such a community is totally beyond the possibility of my imagining.

The Presbyterian churches of Alameda and Placitas, New Mexico, which I served for eight years as missionary and pastor, would be my contrived attempt to build a "beloved community." Both were colossal failures, frauds, neither loving nor beloved. The theory was that our common loyalty to God, our common debt of gratitude to Christ for his sacrifice, would make us "the beloved community." Instead we had backbiting, betrayal and a fear of love that ultimately verged on the comical.

"Love your enemies!" Ha! Communist!

"Love your neighbors!" Ha! They're dirty and don't speak our language.

"Love one another!" Ha! Don't you *dare!*

The phrase "beloved community" puts me on guard, making me a loner, even though I can't shake off some sense of responsibility for other people. I feel like an old Hebrew prophet, estranged from his people by the message that obsesses him—a message about justice and love. A prophet with no "God," but a message nevertheless. And I find I must guard against the Elijah Complex which says, "I alone am left," and the Messiah Complex, which says, "I'll die to save them and they'll not care at all," and even the Noah Complex, which notes, "Being the only one salvaged is no fun either."

Jeremiah was my best mentor back then. He was obsessed with his very unpopular message, that Yahweh was on the side of Nebuchadnezzar and that Jerusalem was doomed. His was a lonely voice. He's the one who can show me what to expect. "Wilt thou be to me like a deceitful brook, like waters that fail?" he complained to the mostly silent God.

But then Jeremiah did receive an answer: "If you have raced with men on foot and they have wearied you, how will you compete with horses? And if in a smooth land you fall down, how will you do in the jungle of the Jordan?"

From time to time I find I need to recall that exchange.

8. HOW IT BEGAN

I spent my childhood and youth encumbered with the conviction that I had to discover God's will and do it. I did well in school, but a course called "Guidance" was very upsetting. Today it would be called "Counseling," if the local budget allowed for it. "Vocational counseling," more specifically, not substance abuse counseling, or divorce counseling. "Guidance" brought up that same question, "What are you going to do with your life?" The pressure was made worse by statements and insinuations, "You're smart enough to do anything, so what will it be?"

Both of my parents had decided early on that I would be a medical doctor. My grandfather had been a doctor; he died young, when my father was five years old. I had been named for him. From this vantage point it is remarkable to follow the course of parental influence on that scared kid, namely me. "The God-stuff will remove any need to consider what he, the victim, wants. We'll use that to bring about the result we want—let's make him a medical missionary."

I doubt that they ever made it that conscious to themselves. And they did not manipulate the thought processes inside my head directly. But they set it up, and it amounted to the same thing. They were "so proud," when I came home from church camp, after throwing into the campfire a heart-shaped "message to God" on which I had written the title of another hymn, "I'll Go Where You Want Me to Go, Dear Lord," and announced, "God has called me to be a medical missionary in Korea." This was 1947 and no one had ever heard of Korea, except a Korean doctor classmate of the local pastor, and a furloughed missionary at that church camp. At any rate, it was settled. The relief was tremendous. Now I knew what "God" wanted me to do.

"God" never spoke directly. I was no good as a mystic. If this process depended on direct revelation, I never had more than that Voice that knew my name. But like any good Protestant, I found "God" in the Bible. I read it, and learned it, learned what was in it, knew it, and tried to let it guide my life. The book is extremely complex, for one who is really reading it, and I was left mostly on my own to do so. The result was that although I was by no means a fundamentalist Bible-pounder in those early days, I was a serious searcher after truth.

I was valedictorian of my high school class, and went to Lafayette College, which was noted then, as now, as an excellent school for preparing premedical students and helping them get into medical school. It appeared that the only way I was going to get in was on the basis of academic grades, since the family had no money and included no influential doctors or lawyers. So I went to work establishing that required academic record. For the first two years, my grades were 95s and 100s. Final grades were given out in multiples of five. 100s were extremely rare, impossible in the humanities, like English literature or history or German. No one could write a perfect essay. But in math and chemistry one could, theoretically, get all the problems right. I did so, and amassed a marvelous collection of 100s.

It was not really a well-rounded education. I was elected to Phi Beta Kappa without having read widely at all. I had two skills: memory for the math and science, and what a fellow student called "intelligent bullshit." I mastered the assigned material, memorized lecture notes, mastered the art of inference, learned to "attack the question," as I came to call it, and got away with it.

I did it all with a sense of obedience—this is what "God" wanted. This is what I needed to do to get on to the next stage. I was under orders, so I did it.

The summer after my freshman year, the war broke out in Korea. Now everyone was hearing of that forsaken place. Most of my high school classmates went into the military. A cousin of mine was one of those captured at that reservoir by the Yalu River border with China.

College students were classified 2-S, meaning military service was deferred as long as we kept our grades up. Premedical students were in no danger of being drafted, but the draft hung over college life like a pall. Borderline academic achievers took hour exams with fear and trembling, and reported that it felt like a kind of lottery in which the losers were taken out and shot. I was unscathed because of the high level of my academic grades, which I achieved with little sense of accomplishment. They were simply required. I felt I was as much under orders as anyone in the United States Armed Forces.

I had no time for anything but the books and the memorizing during the school year, and no money either, if there had been time. There were very few movies. No girls. None of that new invention called "television"—the first time I saw it I felt like an aborigine who couldn't perceive anything sensible when he first saw moving pictures. I couldn't see any picture in the "snow," and I asked a procrastinating student, "What're you watching?" I could literally see nothing but snow. When he said, "The ballgame!" I realized that I could hear Mel Allen's voice, but I still saw no image on the screen. I hurried away to the books and preparations for the next hour exam.

I do remember Bobby Thomson's home run, which defeated the Damn Yankees in the 1951 World Series, heard over the radio in the chemistry lab, where I was solving one of the Qualitative Analysis problems. It was pure delight. Maybe, in spite of everything, there was a glimmer of hope for the self-winding studying machine.

It was during this period that I had my closest contact with fundamentalism. I was part of a college group called Intervarsity Christian Fellowship, directed by fundamentalist pastors in the city. I loved the music, the serious but somehow joyful singing. My serious sense of obedience in preparation for mission made me welcome among them. But I had problems from the beginning. I can now label one of them "rationalism." I did not believe we should turn in our brains at the church door. I agreed with the religion professor who reminded us that we were called to worship God with all our minds, as well as all our soul and all our strength.

Dr. Kunkle, the professor of biology, who didn't believe in "God" at all, had a special eye for me, perhaps because of an earnestness that he liked. He had a profound and lasting effect on me. "I challenge you all," but he was looking at me as he said it, "to muster the courage to follow the truth *wherever it leads.*" There and then, I made a kind of commitment that has penetrated deeper since and has lasted to this day.

9. FUNDAMENTALISM

I became uncomfortable with the fundamentalist group. The theory of evolution was becoming convincing to me, more so as Dr. Kunkle heaped up the evidence in biology and anatomy classes. I had a problem with the Biblical account in Genesis, and the fundamentalists insisted that the stories had to be taken literally. God made the world in six days, not very long ago, they insisted, and no doubts or questions about it were allowed or necessary.

I had asked a fellow worker in the celery patch several years earlier whether or not he believed in evolution. His response triggered something in me, when he stated flatly that Roman Catholics "weren't allowed" to believe in evolution. I resolved that nobody was going to tell me what I was allowed to believe. I would believe according to evidence and experience. And Dr. Kunkle's dare to "follow the truth," follow the evidence wherever it leads, continued to reverberate within me.

In a remarkable religion class in college I first found the concept of myth, and it helped me resolve the conflict between evolution and the first chapters of Genesis. The Bible contained old pre-scientific stories about the origin of things, not unlike the *Just So Stories* of Rudyard Kipling, which I had always enjoyed. The fact that geology and evolution contradicted the literal content of the stories didn't mean that I had to choose between science and revelation. God could and did use myth to reveal his word and will for mankind.

The literalists, who wouldn't admit that *any* of the Bible was myth, had to take a position opposing science and logic and reason. They condemned the open-minded with the label "rationalist." They had verses and quotations to support their view. "For the foolishness of God is wiser than men ... God chose what is foolish in the world to shame the wise." They found and used Tertullian's marvelous statement from the second century: "I believe, because it is absurd." I could not go along with that. My beliefs were not going to be based on a kind of deliberate absurdity.

The concept of myth helped me handle some of the problems in the Biblical text, for example, the contradictions between chapter one and chapter two of Genesis. These are two different stories! Later I used this insight with my own students.

"Little Red Riding Hood took a basket of goodies through the woods toward her grandmother's house. On the way she met the wolf— Wait a minute! It says right here that the wolf died in a cauldron of boiling water in the fireplace of the third little pig's brick house, trying to come down the chimney!"

"Well, but that's a different story!"

"So, the wolf isn't dead?"

"That's not the question. It's a different story. A different myth."

"Oh."

Fundamentalists are not amused by all this fresh insight made available through the notion of myth. They think *myth* means simply that it isn't *true*. They can't imagine God using myth to communicate truth. They believe that whatever the divinely inspired text of the Bible says is literal, historical fact. I was learning to distinguish between truth and fact. There is a kind of truth that has nothing to do with fact—poetry is full of it. So is myth. It was a great relief to me to come to believe that the Bible is full of truth that need not be taken as literal historical fact.

At the same time Dr. Kunkle was teaching me the evidence in biology and anatomy classes, a very gentle Mennonite layman argued with me about evolution. "The devil put those bones in the ground to deceive man." He was referring to the dinosaurs. It was too preposterous for me to consider. By then the devil himself was beginning to look to me like a myth, a metaphor.

Fundamentalists do not believe that they are dealing with myth at all, but fact. If someone suggests that it can't be fact because it is preposterous and impossible, they reply that it is miracle. The greater the absurdity, the more imperative that it be believed. As their position becomes more and more ridiculous, they become more and more shrill, insisting that "God" himself inspired every word of the Bible, as it is, and that it contains no "errors."

Logical questions for intelligent discussion do no good. "You mean the gastric juices of the whale failed to function? And what was Jonah breathing?"

"Do not mock! It was a miracle, God's miracle. God can do anything."

You can't argue with such people. They aren't listening. "It didn't take six days. It took several billion years and is still in process. In the earlier stages there was no such thing as what we call a day, with the earth spinning on its axis in the vicinity of the sun." They simply aren't listening.

A seminary professor used to torment the fundamentalists in his class, one of whom would't even allow the word "metaphor" to describe *any* of the Bible. "So what do you do with Jesus' own statement, 'I am the door'? Are you saying that Jesus is a door, swinging on literal hinges? What could that possibly mean?"

The name "Fundamentalism" was first used among Protestants and is a misnomer. The groups that broke away from the standard-brand Protestant denominations sixty and seventy years ago rallied around five "fundamental" doctrines:

1) The Verbal Inspiration of the Bible,
2) The Virgin Birth of Christ,
3) The Penal-Substitutionary Theory of the Atonement,
4) The Bodily Resurrection of Jesus,
5) The Last Judgment and End of the World.

In my view of things, none of these doctrines is fundamental. Rather more important are truth and trustworthiness, "Justice, mercy and faith," "Faith, hope and love—and the greatest of these is love." At this point in my life I am thankful that I attended the kind of seminary in which I was allowed and encouraged to use reason to find my way clearly and cleanly out of this maze. Let's take a brief look at each of the five "fundamental" doctrines.

1) The Verbal Inspiration of the Bible. A good serious study of the Bible in the original languages of Greek and Hebrew will cure any honest person of the notion of Verbal Inspiration and Absolute Inerrancy. Trying to find the original document, in which "God" supposedly directly inspired, leads to utter frustration. There are literally thousands of variant readings, dozens on a single page, in all the oldest manuscripts in existence, and it is absolutely impossible to say *which* variant reading is the inspired and inerrant one. Also, the differences in style from one author to another make perfect sense and are worth studying if the Bible is a human book, but they are a puzzle if it is a perfectly unified book dictated by a single perfect Divine Being.

Appeals to reason do no good when trying to discuss this with a fundamentalist. Any reference to expertise in the area of mythology counts for nothing. "God said it. I believe it. That settles it."

Now, decades later, after having discarded, or outgrown, the notion of Verbal Inspiration, I nevertheless find myself, as a writer, from time to time held in the grip of the Muse—an old Greek myth that I still use. I am caught by the scruff of the neck and, amid pressures to do a hundred other things, She insists, "Sit thee down, right now, and write more of this." She does not dictate to me, word-by-word, but when I obey her, words flow irresistibly and purposefully out of the end of my pen, often as fast as I can scribble, and I am barely able to keep up with my train of thought.

Where does inspiration come from? I don't know. I doubt if Luke or Jeremiah knew either. It is a mystery, to which the notion of "Verbal Inspiration" does not do justice. And anyway, the people who thought up that notion meant the King James

Authorized Version of 1611, in English, not Luke or John in Greek or Moses and Jeremiah in Hebrew. The oldest manuscripts of the New Testament were unknown to King James' committee of translators, but modern fundamentalists couldn't care less.

2) The Virgin Birth. This is a common element in all the mystery religions, which sprang up as the Roman Empire collapsed. There was considerable competition among those religions for several centuries. Fundamentalists say Christianity won because God's Truth prevailed. Honest doubters suspect that it was the cynical and ruthless use of military power by Constantine and others that won the day. It was no different then than a millennium later, when Christianity replaced Aztec and Toltec and Zapotec beliefs in northern Central America, not because it was true and they were false, but because the Spaniards ruthlessly slaughtered the educated classes of their native western hemisphere victims.

Anyway, the Virgin Birth was a common denominator in all those old mystery religions in the last days of the Roman Empire. The Savior/Hero was a semi-divine being. At the deepest psychological level, the Virgin can represent pure potential, all the unrealized future, all the unmanifested possibilities. Out of that Source the new Hero comes, to challenge Hold-Fast. There are some notions worth pondering here in the myths. But the fundamentalists miss the point of all that, denying that it is myth at all and making it a test of your credulity instead. They keep alive the medieval hostility toward sex and women by maintaining that the myth must be taken literally.

3) The Penal-Substitutionary Atonement. Atonement theories are trying to answer the question, "How does Jesus' dying on the cross save people?" Insistence on this theory of the atonement ignores several other perfectly fine theories, and tries to cram a large and many-faceted idea into a very narrow straightjacket.

The Penal-Substitutionary theory was invented by Anselm back in the 11th century and was a favorite of John Calvin. It says that God is bent on punishing someone, because of "sin," which is taken to be identical to crime. The theory says that Jesus took the rap, and God inflicted the required capital punishment on him. This theory expresses well the tendency of fundamentalists toward legalism, rules, punishment, severity. In my view of it, the theory itself is both illegal and immoral, undermining justice and opening what would be called in current legal jargon a huge loophole. There are other contrasting theories, such as the Moral Influence theory, which emphasizes God's love, but fundamentalists have no time for that. Love is not at the top of their list of virtues.

4) The Bodily Resurrection of Jesus. Fundamentalists don't want to hear about the *meaning* of what some modern theologians have called the "Easter event." They insist that you believe in the literal, factual reassembly of the cells and molecules of Jesus' physical body. The fact that it has been changed into what they call a "spiritual body" doesn't clarify things much.

My own later handling of this one, after I had come to regard *all* of the Bible as myth, is quite personal. I was dead, at one period of my life. I was a zombie and love brought me back to life. Attempts to make the resurrection literal falter for me—I am learning to accept Death as a given, and even a good thing. I have trouble with the Lazarus story, with all its stink and grave-wrappings. But the meaning of it, the application of the idea to my life—I know about that from personal experience.

5) The Last Judgment and End of the World. The God who would do this seems mean to me. I have found the story in which he promised *not* to destroy the world again, as he had in Noah's Flood. But the fundamentalists derive a kind of pleasure from the certainty that the world is doomed and that the vast majority of its inhabitants are condemned to eternal conscious torment. I learned to see this as myth. These judgment ideas could make a thoughtful person reevaluate his life. And looking at judgment socially and

collectively, I think of how "the best country in the world" built enough nuclear bombs to exterminate all life forms on the planet—many times over. Judgment makes sense, after all, but it means that we're in trouble. So here I am, without a God, seeing clearly, like a prophet of old, the end of the world looming, and it's more literal, more factual, than I quite know how to handle.

The fundamentalists insisted that I leave off thinking about all these things, and I refused to do that. I left the group while I was still in college. I am a Rationalist in the sense that the fundamentalists condemn. But the more basic reason for my separating from them was another, more serious, objection. I spotted a kind of inherent mean-heartedness in it. Love was lacking. Any sense of compassion for suffering humanity was lacking. The sovereign "God" they worshipped didn't really like people or the world he had made very much at all.

The love and compassion that they talked about, in connection with Jesus' dying on the cross in order to save those who believed in him, didn't reach far enough to include those who *didn't* believe in him. The message seemed too limited to me. I discovered that the "love" they talked about could go along with racism, militarism and authoritarianism generally with no difficulty. The fundies tended to be quite unloving toward those who had "hardened their hearts" to the point of not agreeing with them. At one point I thought they were making an idol out of their own group and its narrow belief system. When I dropped out, a cloud lifted from me.

Since then I have been an unceasing and unhesitant foe of fundamentalism, first from within the church and then from without. Also, I discovered that not all fundamentalists are Protestant. All the major western religions have a fundamentalist wing, which makes them dangerous to the rest of humanity. They believe that they, and only they, have the truth on their side.

Fundamentalist Jews are extreme right-wing orthodox practitioners, led in Israel by the settlers in the Occupied

Territories. They are utterly uncompromising toward the Palestinians, ready to exterminate them, believing that they were created to be slaves and therefore have no right to object or resist. These people may also be unbending toward other Jews, should they refuse or fail to adhere in some way to the strictest interpretation of traditional Jewish taboos. Some of the fundamentalists deny that these others really are Jews at all.

Fundamentalist Muslims were represented by the late Ayatollah of Iran, although the Afghan mujahideen, to whom recent American governments have given extremely deadly weapons, are more conservative and more dangerous than he was. They leave a bloody trail wherever they go, because they believe that they are right and all the rest of the world is wrong, and they are ready to die for that belief. They have replaced the Communists as the enemy that justifies keeping the American war machine intact.

Fundamentalist Roman Catholics include Pope John Paul II, his Curia, and his fascist supporters all over the world. Opus Dei is a well-known and powerful support group among laymen. Murder and deception are commonly used weapons; one of the more notable recent examples is the murder of John Paul's predecessor, which paved the way for the reforms of Pope John XXIII to be rejected and undone—and it is full steam astern back to the High Middle Ages in theology and in political arrangements. Outside John Paul II's jurisdiction there is no salvation, he says, as if this were the 11th century. There will be no compromise with Liberation Theology. He is quick to ally himself, like other fundamentalists, with Fascist death-squad dictators. When they murder his own liberal bishops, as in El Salvador, he does not object. In fact, he appears glad.

Fundamentalist Protestants have had much publicity lately, not all of it good. Scandals involving TV evangelists have tarnished their reputation somewhat, although less than one would dare expect and hope. Ethical behavior has never been a long suit among them, partly because membership in their group does not depend on behavior but upon professed belief. Dishonest persons can always do well just by saying, "I believe," whether it's true or not. One of their number, a military man, became famous running an illegal, unconstitutional, immoral war from the basement of the White House. He is such an adept liar because he believes that only he and his group are right. Congress is wrong, the majority of the formerly sovereign American people are wrong, and lies to thwart the will of the misguided people are justified.

Fundamentalist Jews, Fundamentalist Muslims, Fundamentalist Roman Catholics, and Fundamentalist Protestants are more like each other, in essential points, than any one of them is like the other branches of each respective religion.

1) They all favor, and practice, the oppression of women, treating them as property.

2) They all use censorship without apology.

3) They are all committed to violence, calling it Holy War.

4) They all confront problems with fanatical closed-minded simple-minded zeal.

5) They have little concern for ethical questions of fairness, or legality, or truth, much less universal love and good will. They tend to be harsh, cruel, unrelenting and mean.

6) They all display the conviction that one's own group is right, and they hate "heretics" as much or more than the simply unwashed unbelievers.

This is the arrogance of those who really know: "We are right; they are wrong. They live in error, in darkness; they are deceived and deceiving. We have the Truth, the Whole Unchangeable Truth that will not shift with time nor with widened or altered perspective. Those benighted persons do not know the Truth and need for us to tell it to them. They are lost. If they don't believe us when we tell them the Truth, then they are doubly lost."

The group is held together by a commonly-held belief system.

Members who stop believing, for whatever reason, are cast into outer darkness. Open-minded persons are despised as unbelievers and bad examples and bad teachers.

I recall the treatment I received from the Intervarsity Christian Fellowship when my perspective widened and changed. I came to realize that the little creed I had been taught as a child did not contain all truth, that I didn't know everything, that, in fact, I knew extremely little. Finally I reached the point where I was sure of only one thing, namely that I did *not* know. It was extremely liberating to find a teacher, and then later to become the same kind of teacher, who could exclaim, "Gosh! It beats me! I don't know! Let's check it out. What do *you* think? What do you know about it?"

I came to believe that fundamentalism is a form of idolatry. The idol is "God." The belief system encourages people to believe that they and God constitute the good guys, the good side in a great cosmic struggle. They then tend to believe that they can do no wrong in defense of that supposed "good." It is pure ego, pure selfishness. "God will punish them. God will get me what I want. God will protect me. God will prove I'm right." "God," in this view, is like a kind of secret weapon, which most don't have, poor dumb wicked sinners that we are.

Fundamentalists too easily resort to lying and then murdering in the name of "God." Since logic was thrown out long ago, and love, too, there's no way to appeal to them to bring them to their senses. They are obsessed with "God," and that God of theirs is cruel, ruthless, heartless and bloody. It is war-thinking. They tend to be pro-war people. Their songs and prayers are full of military imagery. They use war analogies to explain things. They do pick up some of this from our militarized culture, to be sure, but it is native to their belief system at the same time.

For fundamentalists there is no overarching Truth, no Cosmic Ethical Source. The word "God" could refer to precisely that, for some thoughtful people, but the fundamentalists have limited "God" to a secret weapon for use in their paltry fights. There is no sensitivity regarding what it would be like to be the other guy—a black person, a poor person, a battered woman, an Asian, a communist, a dolphin, a Martian.

I wonder what Jesus would say to them. "Why do you call me, 'Lord, Lord!' and not do what I say?" What he said was, "Love one another. Love your neighbor. Love your enemies." The white supremacy, capital punishment, sexist, anti-welfare, pro-war, we're-the-best nonsense is a parody of what the texts say the fundamental heart of Christianity should be.

The meaning of Jesus' parables of judgment do not help a fundamentalist at this point. The stories could lead a thoughtful person to examine his life and try to make it worth living, but instead fundamentalists tend to place themselves in a smug group. After death they'll go to be "with God," in the bosom of Abraham, on the other side of that great gulf fixed. There they'll feel separated and superior—among the sheep despising the goats, with the saved looking down on the lost. They are not humbled by the mysteries of grace and forgiveness. The fundamentalists miss the point of the gospel, and then dare to call their small ego-riddled beliefs "fundamental."

My experience in that fundamentalist group as a youth leads me to be hopeful about individuals. One can become unstuck, and go on through that process. I am especially hopeful about young ones who are not inherently mean-hearted. I'm willing to predict that they'll become sick of all the hatred and the violence and proceed toward maturity.

As for the leaders of the movement I am less hopeful. I do not believe that they really believe the things they say and preach on television. I suspect that they do not believe much of anything, except perhaps that they are superior to others. I do not believe that it is possible to hold inside the same brain their supposed belief in a Just and Judging God, and the knowledge of what they've come to stand for: war, gang-rape, mass murder, obliteration napalm and phosphorous anti-personnel bombing, assassination, lies, lies, lies. The two images don't fit together. I conclude that they do not really believe in a *just* God at all.

10. THE BIBLE

Having shaken off fundamentalism, I found myself thoroughly enjoying my ongoing studies of the Bible. The old phrase, "written by the finger of God," was not to be taken literally. No organization would determine what I was to be allowed to believe. I would follow the truth wherever it led. About then I found the poem, "Invictus," and recognized the mood: "I am the master of my fate, I am the captain of my soul." I wasn't quite that free yet, but I was on my way.

I can see now a long, relentless, inexorable process, set in motion by small insignificant-looking things. You repudiate the authority of a church you're not a part of, and you can someday repudiate the authority of the church you are a part of. You repudiate a mean-hearted fundamentalist evangelist, and you can someday repudiate the authority of a seemingly loving father who says he wishes you well, but means it only if you do what he says. You repudiate a stand-in for God, and someday you can repudiate—look out!—God Himself. You decide you want to decide for yourself, and you may very well get your chance.

I was drawn to the concept of myth, and attracted to a serious study of the Bible from this new point of view. Meanwhile I had a problem. I had earned the grade-point average required to obtain an acceptance into a medical school, the University of Pennsylvania, where my grandfather had attended half a century before. But I hated the prospect of it. I did not want to become a doctor. My fellow pre-med students would have sold their souls to have what I didn't want—that acceptance to Penn Medical School. I was not able at the time to define exactly what it was that I didn't like about it. My professors were all very supportive, and I did very well in chemistry and biology classes, but I hated it.

From this long perspective I would say I was rebelling against parental pressure to go into medicine. There's no question that it was their idea. My father's father had been a country doctor, who died of Bright's disease at age 35, when my father was five years old. His family assumed he would become a doctor, but he disappointed them with the extremely lame excuse that he fainted at the sight of blood. They did get to him, nevertheless, somehow, because he passed the expectation on to me, and my mother went along with the idea.

So my resistance to medical school was my rebellion, timed also to coincide with my decision to get married, far too early and against everyone's wishes and advice. The decision to go to seminary was a sort of compromise. I loved the languages, which most of my fellow seminarians hated, and I loved the mythology, although I certainly wasn't ready to call it that at that time, not all of it, at any rate.

In some ways it's sort of humorous, what I was able to convince myself of. It had seemed earlier that God had a very specific plan as to what I was supposed to do with my life— medical missionary in Korea. Now I had to talk God out of that, and get his "permission to go to seminary." I wonder that I was able to pull it off. But remember, the Voice never spoke, never spelled out any of it. I had been filling in blanks for a long time. While we were at it, "God" also granted permission for me to get married at that time.

In seminary, my specialty was Biblical studies in the original languages. I didn't have to jettison the Bible and God in the name of Truth, after all. Yet. I do see the beginning of another inexorable process, however. I can hear the fundamentalists taunting, "You start throwing out chunks of God's holy Inspired Word, and where does it end? First, the beginnings of Genesis—then what next? The miracles of Moses? Then what? The miracles of Elijah and Daniel and Jesus? Then what? The story of the death and resurrection of our dear Lord and precious Savior Jesus Christ? No—you have to keep all of it, or you lose all of it." It was, indeed, a downhill slide.

In seminary I was fascinated by all that symbolism in the footnotes of the Greek text, which delineated all the variant readings of all the extant manuscripts. My fundamentalist classmates were extremely upset by this, but I loved Vaticanus, and Alexandrinus and Sinaiticus, those oldest manuscripts. The first half of any exegesis paper was called "establishing the text"—going through all those variants and deciding which text one was going to translate and interpret. I gobbled it up, unperturbed by the fact that if God *had* verbally inspired an original text, it was lost forever.

In the Old Testament there was not quite such a huge mass of confusion, but there was one big historical fact in the way of locating a sure and certain original text. As the rabbi read the passage in the synagogue, after the return from Exile, when the Book began to take on its magical authority, the rabbi would sometimes read something different from what was written. *K'thib* means "written." *Q'eré* means "called." *K'thib* and *Q'eré*—it became a magic phrase for us bewildered young scholars. The kicker was that later manuscripts were not always copied exactly as before—sometimes the *Q'eré* replaced the *K'thib*—and how were we to know?

The most common instance of this had to do with the Divine Name, YHWH. YHWH was the *K'thib*. No rabbi, nobody ever, would pronounce it. We don't even know now how they did pronounce it, before this superstition about the magic name caught on. The *Q'eré* was *'Adonai* (Lord). So when the rabbi came to YHWH in the text, he read *'Adonai*. Then in later manuscripts, when scribes added the vowel points, which weren't in the older texts, they inserted the vowel points of *'Adonai* into YHWH. That's the origin of the name "Jehovah," which we can be sure was not the original pronunciation of YHWH. You can tell I'm still fascinated. I suppose not everyone is.

The study of the original languages allowed us to begin to get the feel of the personalities of the authors. The poetry of Job is different from the narrations of I Samuel, just as the poetry of Shakespeare is different from the narrations of Mark Twain—just as different. The simplicity of the Gospel of John is quite a contrast from the tortured complexity of some of the letters of Paul. Paul probably did not write the letter to the Hebrews, based on its simple directness. The personalities of the human authors began to show, for me. The experiences, the historical settings of the authors, became essential to an understanding of what the text might mean.

But a process of erosion had begun. The pre-scientific statements of Genesis had to be reinterpreted. Meanwhile, scientific geology faded from prominence as the great yardstick by which the text was to be evaluated. Myth became the clue. What is the purpose of the myth? What values are being declared? Who is saying this, and why? Once analysis starts, there's no stopping it.

I found myself looking at the Bible in a new way. It was a marvelously variegated source of *human* experience, not a puzzling exposé of the Divine Will. *That* remained as enigmatic as ever. Without setting it down deliberately, I found myself using yardsticks of my own to evaluate the stories and poems and letters and lists that make up the Bible. I liked best what was most human and most honest.

In the Old Testament, I had little respect for, and finally little interest in, those sections that support the authority of priests and kings. I was on the side of the prophets. They were lonely outsiders, thundering and wailing and sometimes whimpering, in the name of YHWH, in the name of truth and humanity. The prophets were the authors or originators of much of the material, although the priests got in the final word in the late "redactions" of the text. I learned to smell out that priestly influence and repudiate it.

It amazed me how frank parts of the Old Testament remained, even after that priestly meddling. The great heroes had bad "warts and all" on their portraits. Abraham lied about his wife Sarah, calling her his sister, hoping to save his skin. Jacob was a cheating, lying scoundrel. His sons were no better. Joseph was insufferably smug. Moses was a coward—"Oh, Lord, send some other person!" Joshua was a genocidal maniac. David couldn't keep his hands off other men's wives. Solomon had so many wives, one had to question his basic intelligence—he certainly didn't write Proverbs or Ecclesiastes, which are called Wisdom Literature! Rehoboam was a small-minded fool. Ahab, Josiah, Hezekiah, Zedekiah—all had feet of clay. But, when you read it carefully, you find the Bible telling it frankly.

The prophets became my heroes, and in a deep sense they still are. Elijah challenged the power of King Ahab and Queen Jezebel. Amos insisted that justice for all was more important than priestly ritual. Hosea learned and taught about mercy and the transformative power of suffering. Ezekiel showed that YHWH had survived the fall of Jerusalem, making him different from the other land-based war gods of other nations. Second Isaiah challenged the people in exile to become God's instrument to do good to all the world—they were the Chosen People, not because they were better, but because they had a special mission.

Jeremiah became my favorite. Called at the time of the decline and fall of the last surviving Hebrew state, the tiny kingdom of Judah, he had this very unpopular message: Since justice and honesty were not the rule in Judah, YHWH had changed sides and was fighting for the Babylonians—and the fall of Jerusalem to the Babylonian Emperor *was God's will*, in order to purify his people. That subversive message got Jeremiah into endless serious trouble, and sometimes he complained honestly. But his "call," his message, prevailed: "If I say, 'I will not mention him, or speak any more in his name,' there is in my heart as it were a burning fire shut up in my bones, and I am weary with holding it in, and I cannot."

That still moves me. I don't believe there is any "him" in it, anymore—not YHWH, no "God." But about Truth, Justice, Fairness, Equality, whatever is at the bottom of it all—those slogan words are all too cheap, too tarnished, too contaminated by misuse, and "God" is far too glib—whatever it is, if I try to shut up about it, go about my life as if nothing at all mattered, "there is in my heart as it were a burning fire shut up in my bones, and I become weary with trying to hold it in, and I cannot." So my poems and plays and short stories and novels all pick up another element, not mere entertainment, some kind of warning, some kind of challenge, some kind of protest.

Most of this reevaluation of the Bible took place while I was a Presbyterian missionary-pastor in New Mexico. I didn't keep the process a deep dark secret from the congregations, as most of my colleagues did. Only a few of them were experiencing this anyway—they were operating religious organizations, and used the Bible as a source of texts for sermons, and used the sermon to hold together a social gathering. I called myself "teaching elder," and used the sermon to teach, and shared in my teaching what was most important to me. Most didn't hear it, or make anything much of it, to be sure, but some did.

Religion itself became for me a major problem. The people wanted me to be a priest, but I was a prophet. One lady said it openly, in the last stages, "We don't want *truth*. We want comfort."

I liked the anti-religious parts of the Old Testament best. Ecclesiastes became a favorite—that wise old cynic, who had no time for empty phrases and puffed-up egos.

The Book of Jonah became pivotal. Since leaving ecclesiastical organizations, I have worked it over at length, preparing a full-length play. It has had many titles: *When You Get It Done*, was first. Then simply, *Regurgitation*. Now I call it, *The Healing of Jonah*. My clue is that the prophet in the story of Jonah is not Jonah, but the *author* of the Book of Jonah.

I invent him, and call him Sidekick. The brains of the outfit is his wife, Lady Sidekick. The two of them ply Sidekick's trade of scribe—writer!—on the Memphis-to-Nineveh caravan route. They are squatting on a Forest Service campground, near the beach. A huge fish is washed ashore. With it comes a half-drowned man, Jonah, on his way to Nineveh. The Sidekicks question him and learn that Jonah's God-obsession makes him a much meaner person than he would otherwise be. He hears a voice. His interpretation of what the voice wants him to do accents his own mean-spirited nature. Assorted camel-drivers, Emperor Ashurbanipal—he of the library—and the emperor's gorgeous, philosophically curious daughter Ishtar aid in Lady Sidekick's project of healing Jonah of his God-obsession.

In the final scene, Lady Sidekick agrees that Sidekick should write it all down. "And leave the whale out of it!" she barks at the end. But, of course, we know he does not, and we have all the subsequent confusing nonsense about Jonah and the Whale. So, I'm still trying to salvage, and not only for myself, what I think is a remarkably frank, funny, anti-religious story, right there in the Bible.

In the New Testament, I became disgusted with Paul, the Ecclesiasticator. For a while I wished we could get past Paul and back to Jesus, but I finally decided that it's not possible. Jesus, as rabbi and yogi, itinerant healer and prophet, is an admirable character, I believe, but all the effort to make him the central figure in a new mystery religion seemed to me, in the end, unfortunate and, given all the slaughter in his name since, downright disgusting. I liked the Letter of James, but wondered why it was in the New Testament at all. Certain sayings of Jesus, including the Sermon on the Mount, seemed prophetic and true.

I used to wonder when the Christian Church got "off the track." The exercise was started by the notion hidden in the word "Reformation," as in "the Protestant Reformation," that the church had fallen into error, and prophets like me were called by God to get it back on track. But as I traced it, the trouble, the error, went back further and further in time—back before the invention of the Papacy at the time of Leo the Great, the Bishop of Rome who had to deal with Attila the Hun (I didn't believe for a moment that Peter was ever Bishop of Rome, or Pope); back before the Emperor Constantine made Christianity legal and then established it as the only legal religion for the Empire (faith is not a matter of legality); back before the invention of the clergy and bishops. I had the free-thinker's conviction that all believers were equal, that there was no rank, not legitimately, that rank was an invention of men grabbing power. I was failing as a clergyman because I did not believe in the office I held, did not believe that ordination effected any change at all, even though the majority of people in the congregations *did* believe that I was supposed to be a better Christian than they.

I finally traced the error back to the very beginning of Christianity. Bishops are referred to in the New Testament, but worse than bishops and rank, the initial error that I found was right there at the beginning. Most of the disciples of Jesus changed Jesus from Example and made him Substitute. All the theological argument about his divinity had to do with this. Instead of a teacher and a healer, who taught his disciples that they, too, could heal and move mountains, they made him into a divine sacrifice, who died for those who believed certain rather preposterous things about him. His divinity was required in order to give his sacrifice the power to bring about the salvation of the believers. If he isn't divine, his dying is not a sacrifice. I saw his life as a challenge, and a warning: Are you ready to suffer the consequences of truth-telling? Look clearly and then speak carefully, because here you see the consequences!

I still believe that Jesus is quite remarkable and admirable, as Example. But since I had ceased being interested in religion as such—that is, as a priestly scheme to help people feel "saved," enabling them to persist in what Nietzsche long ago called "the slave mentality"—Jesus as Sacrifice turned me off. The church, as I came to see it, and still see it, is the caretaker of that religion, and not much interested in encouraging anyone to follow Jesus as Example. When such followers do turn up, they are always in trouble. Most are killed or expelled as heretics. A few, like Teresa de Avila and Francis of Assisi, are made into saints, so they need not be taken seriously as additional Examples.

So, in the New Testament the worst religion-makers were Paul and the author of the Epistle to the Hebrews. The gospels, in their final form, contained older anti-religious material but also plenty of Jesus-as-God stuff. The Book of Acts showed the transition from stunned followers of an executed Jesus who believed that he had risen from the dead, to a church led by missionary Paul, who was spreading a new mystery religion all over the eastern Mediterranean and all the way to Rome.

Early sections of the gospels, especially "Logia"—words, teachings of Jesus—had to be separated from the work of the ecclesiasticating redactor. All my studies of the New Testament in Greek enabled me to make a kind of sense of all that, but did not enhance my loyalty to any ecclesiastical institution.

11. SAVED BY THE GLANDS

Married! Where'd that fool notion come from? What happened to the self-winding studying machine? Well, a funny thing happened on the way to the Lafayette College Choir concert.

All my short life I had been a failure with girls. It felt as if there was something the matter with me. I was skinny and ugly, a runner more than a fighter, too serious, with wire-rimmed glasses and crooked teeth. Thinking back on it all, I am grateful that my parents did not teach me to hate and despise my own body. There was enough nudism, and enough earthy humor in that family that I didn't inherit deep psychological self-hate problems. But girls shunned me, and I was the butt of more than my share of puberty jokes from male peers, as I struggled to learn the names of things and to comprehend internal processes that seemed full of power and mystery.

After feeling betrayed by a high school girl that I really cared about, I put all that on hold for several years, thinking it was part of the obedience I was offering to God. There was no way I could get through all that school and work that was set before me with a girlfriend! I funneled all the psychosexual energy that was seething beneath the surface into books and formulae and hour exams.

At the end of my first year at Lafayette College, I joined the college choir. It was a great outlet for libido—an all-men's school, with an all-men's choir, strong young voices getting good training. We did plenty of sacred music, so-called, but we also did a lot of popular romance. The choir director loved Fred Waring and his arrangements. We belted out "Let there be—LIGHT!" from *The Creation* by Richter. And we also did "You'll Never Walk Alone."

The choir toured all over the area giving concerts. On a fatal spring afternoon and evening, we went to Beaver College, an all-girls' school in the Philadelphia suburbs. A dinner was held for choir members and Beaver students, and blind dates had been arranged for a dance after.

It is strange to remember how I knew in advance, somehow, that I was going to meet someone who "would be important in my life," at that concert. I had not had anything that could be called a date in over two years. I had sworn off women. Yet I went with a strange sense of openness, of being ready for this new adventure, before it started. It is still quite mysterious.

We sat together at the dinner, before the blind dates were announced and couples paired off. We liked each other instantly. She told later how she hadn't wanted to go, and was pushed into going by family members at home. We decided that she should speak to the lady with the list and get the official Blind Date arrangement changed, so we'd be together for that whole evening—and the thing went into motion.

We liked each other. Neither had ever felt so liked before, so affirmed, so approved of. We arranged additional dates, began to exchange letters, and the thing became serious early on. When we started to touch one another—well, it was necessary to change plans, so they would include our getting married.

The commitment was quickly made and unconditional. We were all old-fashioned enough to accept the notion, which now seems bizarre, that the sexual attraction should remain frustrated until we were married. Times have changed.

We had to get parental permission, which wasn't easy, since my folks sensed their dream of "our son, the doctor" going out the window. The decision to marry was linked, strangely, to the decision to go to seminary instead of medical school. For me the tricky part was talking "God" into it. It seemed I was asking him to change his mind. I wasn't called to be a celibate, chronically unhappy medical missionary. I was being called to be a joy-filled, more-aware-than-ever, merely human being, who was going to learn Hebrew and Greek and many other mythically wonderful things, with this marvelous companion!

I found verses, and other help, for my argument. Dietrich Bohnhoeffer had written from the Nazi prison that it was foolish and wrong for Christians to try to be "more pious than God." God had *invented* sexuality and families. I even made a case, for my own inner use, of the fact that something like sexual attraction could be perceived at the bottom of things in each of my special fields of study.

Chemical valence looked like sexual attraction. Chlorine atoms really *wanted* another electron to complete that outer ring. Sodium atoms really *wanted to give away* that lonely extra electron on its outer ring—oh, I knew that feeling!

Biological evolution took place over the eons because of an incredible amount of copulation that went on and on, all the time, and still goes on—up and down and all over the family tree of life forms that are always mating, always recombining, always exchanging "seed." I was just joining a process that was bigger and older than I.

So, we were married, and I made plans to go to seminary. Some of the prophets had wives—and now I had one. The effect on me was wholly good. I softened, I learned about pleasure, joy, fun! I learned to care, really, about someone else. I learned to do for someone besides myself and this strange obsession with mission. I learned about dirty diapers, about providing shoes and milk, about picnics and toys, songs and languages, mental illness and many more things. I had gone into motion, at the start, thinking life was a mission, a task, but I began at this point to learn that it could also be a dance, with no meaning beyond what it is *at this moment*.

I thought I had pulled a fast one on God, getting him to "change his mind" about me and that mission, but life was doing its thing on me, instead.

12. CHURCH HISTORY

My seminary training included a frank and thorough study of what was called "church history." It fascinated me and provided me with a remarkably complete picture of the history of Europe since about 100 A.D. and of North America since 1600 A.D. However, that study did not fortify any personal loyalty to the institutional church. Before it was over I was saying things like, "One of the great antidotes to an infection of Christianity is a strong dose of the study

How God Died

of the history of Christianity."

The beginnings in the ancient Roman Empire were nothing to be proud of. Slaves seeking cosmic solace and thoughtful persons seeking some overarching meaning in a culture built on violence and injustice—these made up the followers of the new mystery religion called Christianity. The divine being, son of God, born of a virgin, who died to save his followers, was a common figure in *all* mystery religions of that time. Gilbert Murray was a scholar of Greek thought in the ancient period, when the Greeks did the thinking and the Romans did the practical execution, like war and road-building. In his book, *The Five Stages of Greek Religion*, he summarized the fascination with mystery religions on the part of thoughtful people as, "The Failure of Nerve."

For three centuries, it was unclear which of several of these mystery religions was going to win out. Constantine cleared that up. The details of the story are quite revealing. Christianity didn't win because it was *true*, but because the winner of the battle to control the Empire was a man who believed that Christ and his symbol, the Cross, fought and conquered beside him. Christ was a war god, like YHWH in the early sections of the Old Testament—for example, in the time of Joshua and the Conquest of Canaan.

It was war, not truth, that enabled Christianity to win. It was killing, not loving and serving, that put Christianity in the position to run that huge collapsing empire in 313 A.D. And the rest of the story, beginning immediately, consists of more killing —of heretics at first and continually since (Arians, Nestorians, Albigensians, Waldensians, Unitarians, Quakers), of opponents (pagans, witches, "savages," Saracens, Aztecs, Incas), and of each other (Eastern Orthodox, Lutheran, Calvinist, modern liberation theologians). It is a disgusting bloody story.

The history of the Papacy is a marvelous study in deceit, betrayal, torture and slaughter. For those of us brought up in little rural churches, ready to believe in love and peace and service, all this new knowledge of the history of the churches was a source of pain and anger. They sucked us into the service of an institution that can never clean the blood from its hands, nor from its soul.

I remember my chagrin, reading Kenneth Scott Lattourette's *The History of Christianity*, upon finding his account of the first time that Christian soldiers went to battle against *other* Christian soldiers and civilians. That was *before* Constantine, in wars the results of which matter very little to any of us now. But something very basic was betrayed.

The Crusades were a wicked mockery of the church's supposed message. To free holy places from unbelievers, by killing those unbelievers—is that what this is really all about? The height of cynicism was reached when the crusading army went out of its way to sack Constantinople, which was as Christian as Rome. Western Civilization has not yet finished paying for the hatred caused by the Crusades and their impact on the Near East.

We studied the Protestant Reformation. It seemed so justified, given the abuses of the Latin Church. Luther seemed so right, in denouncing indulgences. Did anyone really believe that God's good will and forgiveness could be bought, at bargain prices? "Justification by faith *alone*"—Luther added that last word, since it isn't in the Biblical text—it seemed to be the very heart of the gospel.

And then we read of the Peasant Revolt, and Luther's response to it. He took the side of the princes and the landlords, even though the cause of peasants and laborers was obviously just and would have had the support of Amos or any of the prophets of the Old Testament. But no. I was well aware of my peasant-proletariat roots, Pennsylvania farmers and Scottish coal miners. But no. Luther thundered against the rebels, encouraging wholesale slaughter of them. Lutheranism, and Protestantism generally, has never since been able to remove the stench of its instinctive alliance with The Establishment.

The story in North America is not much different. "Wilderness Zion" in Massachusetts, and "The Holy Experiment" in Pennsylvania, were set up to give Christianity a fresh start in "the New World." The story becomes a nonstop record of genocide, slavery and ecological destruction. The continent certainly would be healthier if the Christians had never come. Native cultures were ruthlessly destroyed.

Cotton Mather gave public thanks to Almighty God for the plague that wiped out entire tribes in New England. William Penn's sons cheated the Lenni Lenape of entire counties of land in one day's operation, called "The Walking Purchase." In areas to the south and west, the Spanish Empire spread with missionary zeal, destroying native culture, including written languages and lore that cannot even be imagined now. Whole populations were enslaved and worked to death in mines and fields. It was genocide, on both continents, in the name of the Prince of Peace.

An anecdote caught my attention and has stuck with me. An Aztec chief asked his tormentors if there were Christians in heaven. He was being offered the chance to be strangled before burning, if he would become a Christian, so he could go to heaven. When assured that heaven was full of Christians, that that's where they went when they died, he said, "Light the fire! I don't want to go where any of them are."

Slavery was endorsed by the Christians, Catholic and Protestant, and the quantity of misery on three continents remains incalculable, and not yet repaid.

I began to wonder whether I really wanted to represent all this wickedness in the world. I felt guilty just being a fellow Christian, with all those evil-doers wearing the same label.

13. THE ORIGINAL LIE

I did the seminary class work at a slightly slower pace than my classmates. I had been appointed "student pastor" of a rural parish in northern New Jersey and moved my family into the manse there. Our daughter had been born during that first fall quarter of my school work, and we moved in a raging snowstorm just in time for Christmas. From there I commuted 67 miles one way to classes in Princeton, in the days before limited access freeways. From this perspective, it seems merely stupid, but I did it willingly, gladly, even proudly. I could combine obedience to God with a family of my own and the fun of studying matters that fascinated me.

I preached every Sunday, conducted youth classes, visited the sick, buried the dead. I did everything a pastor does except conduct the sacraments (baptism and communion) and officiate at weddings (a state function). One had to be ordained to do those things.

All through seminary I balked at the idea of ordination. I did not believe that clergy were in any way different from or separated from the people. I had an extremely egalitarian form of Christianity in my heart. I liked the Quaker system, at least in theory—no clergy at all.

At the end of three years I was not through with the seminary course, since I took fewer classes at a time, with all the commuting and the parish work. I had another year to go. And then a unique opportunity opened up. The Board of Foreign Missions, as it was then called, offered a year's study fellowship in Madrid, Spain, to a "mature" seminary student. The study part would be to learn the Spanish language and write a thesis. The mature part involved serving as a sort of chaperon for two Junior-Year-Abroad college students, since the full-time fraternal worker assigned to Madrid was going to be back in the U.S. on furlough. I had a wife and daughter, and my wife was pregnant. I had served three years as

How God Died

student pastor. I was very young still, but perhaps I was more mature than some. At any rate we applied for the fellowship, and received it, and spent a full year in Madrid.

We all became bilingual. I had two tutors a day that summer. By the last Sunday in August I was able to preach in Spanish in one of the churches of the Spanish Evangelical Church. I attended the University of Madrid, earning the Diploma of Hispanic Studies. I adapted for the first time to a large city, and to life under a Fascist Catholic police-state dictatorship, in which one tolerated subtle and not-so-subtle surveillance from the Guardia Civil. I taught English to fifth graders in an illegal Protestant school. I learned much about cultural diversity.

Then I returned to Princeton Seminary for my final year of study, and to the Sussex County parish 67 miles away. Our third child was born that winter in another raging snowstorm. As the end of the school year loomed, our family went into serious crisis.

Where, after all this preparation, does the Lord want us to serve him? I was not going to stay on full-time where I had served part-time for four years. I had assumed there would be some kind of assignment offered from the Board of Foreign Missions, somewhere in the Spanish-speaking world, but nothing came up. It took a while for me to grasp it, but I finally realized that the Board regarded me as something of a potential troublemaker, given my analysis of the conditions inside the Spanish Evangelical Church, which I had been a part of, and careful observer of, during my year in Spain. I had written the required thesis while there, and in it I told chapter and verse of the history and current conditions, calling things by their correct names. Not everything was sweetness and light.

The Spanish Evangelical Church consisted of about 10,000 members in the entire country. A couple dozen pastors led the group. Some were in their eighties, the others were in their twenties and thirties. All the rest, except one, had been killed off during and after the Spanish Civil War. That one had spent the war on a Nazi gunboat off the coast. He ruled the church with the same dictatorial power that Franco used to rule Spain.

The Board forbade that I ever publish that paper, and I wonder now, after all that has happened, why I obeyed. At any rate no call came from the Board of Foreign Missions. I made myself available to parishes all over New Jersey, thinking I would enroll for additional study if a call came. None did.

Meanwhile the family was going deeper into crisis. My wife slipped into a form of mental illness, which frightened her and all of us. It started as postpartum distress and depression, but became more serious, and finally threatening, she thought, to the baby. She went into therapy, which was traumatic in itself back in those benighted days.

A seminary class visited the Board of National Missions. One of the officials latched on to me, with my bilingual abilities and experience, and wanted to send me to a three-point Spanish-speaking parish in New Mexico. I balked, for reasons that are still not clear. Contrariness, pure and simple, maybe. New Mexico? I learned *Castellano*, in order to go to New Mexico? Where was it, even? I had never been west of Chicago.

The family tension grew. Where will we be in six weeks? Graduation is only a month away! The mental illness worsened. I was in a class called Pattern of Life, which consisted of much reading, and an analysis of one's autobiography, seeking the pattern. The professor believed implicitly that God had a plan for each human life, and so, for that matter, did I. I had to find the plan. I mean I really had to find it, and pretty quick. I went to talk to the professor. "Board of Foreign Missions?" he asked.

"Nothing."

"What about the Board of National Missions?"

"Well, they have something out in New Mexico, but I don't want to go there, with my wife sick, and all."

His eyebrow went up. "You say your life is locked? Well, who locked it?"

I left him and went to a pay phone and called the Board offices in New York, and told them I was going to New Mexico. When I told my wife what I had done, she relaxed visibly and began to mend immediately and was well before we arrived in New Mexico. The rest of my Pattern of Life included the theme of rural parish work, and the blessing of family and intimacy, and the virtue of obedience to a call. I was really ready and eager to serve the Lord in New Mexico. I went out there, like Abraham went out, "not knowing where he was going." When the Board changed the destination from Mora, Holman and Chacon to Alameda, Placitas and Bernalillo, I shrugged. The map meant little, since I had never seen any of it.

There was one little catch. I couldn't go serve my unseen parish without being ordained. Well, in comparison to my eagerness to go, my ecclesiastical doubts about the efficacy of "the laying on of hands" carried little weight. So I underwent the Presbytery examination.

It was an all-day, formal oral examination, by a committee made up mostly of young pastors. I did very well in Bible and church history and "polity," that is, how the Presbyterian Church is organized. The interesting part was theology. I knew the history, the schools, the definitions. I knew Augustine and Calvin and Schopenhauer and Schleiermacher. When it came to what I personally believed, we hit a snag. I did not believe in the Virgin Birth. I thought it was an anti-woman, anti-sex doctrine, cooked up by frustrated celibates, and that it detracted from the full humanity of Jesus. "Oh, that's what we think, too," one of the examiners said.

"Aha!" said I. "So what should I say when you ask me, in the ordination ceremony, whether I believe that the Westminster Confession of Faith contains that system of doctrine taught in the Holy Scriptures?" The Westminster Confession of Faith was written in 1643, as part of the Cromwellian Revolution in England! The ordination questions were meant to cement modern loyalty to *that*. "I don't believe the Scriptures teach a system of doctrine at all—the Scriptures are far too complex for that. And just for instance, I don't believe personally in the Doctrine of the Virgin Birth. So, should I say, No?"

They all smiled, looking at each other. "Oh, no, don't do that," one said. "That would stop proceedings."

"So I should say Yes, meaning No."

They looked sheepish. "We all did it. We're working hard to change the ordination ceremony. You can help us."

It was subtle. Guys I liked, who wanted to be honest but weren't being so, were encouraging me to join them. But the only way I could join them was to be as dishonest as they. It was going to be called "boring from within." It was later going to be compared to the French Underground: "Smile at the Nazis all day, and blow 'em up at night."

From this perspective, the dishonesty stands out more than anything else. My view of all this will be colored forever by the sense of relief, of freedom, when I could at last, upon quitting and demitting ten years later, be honest again.

14. BORING FROM WITHIN

I was "boring from within" from the very beginning. I was convinced the church needed reforming, and had needed it since before I joined. From the position of clergyman, attained by answering "Yes" when I really meant "No" to that key question in the ordination ceremony, I worked hard to undermine the role and image of the clergy.

I knew that clergy were not different from laity in any perceptible way. I knew, from experience, that ordination did not change anything at all, just as baptism hadn't earlier. The same confusion of mixed motives, hormones, pet ideas, bad buttons, broken resolutions and fresh attempts to do better dominated my life and those of my colleagues and all the laity. We were all "merely human."

I was appointed "missionary" to three tiny congregations in New Mexico. I preached in Spanish, conducted pastoral calls in Spanish, except with younger families who were more comfortable in English, and entered into the work of the Presbytery of Rio Grande.

Over the years the churches grew, younger families came in, and the congregations became less dependent on National Missions support. The work became bilingual, because the younger members were not fluent in Spanish. Elderly speakers of only Spanish resented the change and blamed me for it. A great deal of energy was wasted on the language barrier. I did the best I could. There was a period when I prepared my sermon, and didn't know which language I was going to preach it in until I counted the monolingual people, of each sort, during the singing of a hymn. Now it seems silly that this constituted such a difficulty, and that I, who loved the Spanish language so much, got credit in the minds of so many for doing away with it.

At one point, the elderly Session (local church ruling body) was on the attack, asserting that English should be *forbidden* in worship services. I told them, remarkably calmly, *"El último pastor de habla española que ustedes van a tener soy yo."* It was true—I was the last Spanish-speaking pastor that church would ever have.

But my leadership was undermined partly by my own disbelief in the position I held. I did not believe that my prayers were more efficacious than those of others. I did not believe that I should dictate policy at session meetings. I believed the people should make decisions, guided by what was clearly right and fair to all and consonant with the Christian ideal of love.

I hated the title "Reverend," never used it, would not allow it as a form of address. The startled reactions I provoked were sometimes amusing, and sometimes not. I was often dismayed and disgusted at the consternation my behavior caused in fellow clergy. They seemed to like being called "Reverend." I did a Biblical word-study.

The word "reverend" does not appear in modern English translations. It appears once in the King James Authorized Version of 1611. One verse in an obscure Psalm, not one of those we have all memorized, says, "Holy and reverend is his name." I looked up the Hebrew. The word being translated "reverend" by the Elizabethan committee means "dreadful," "inspiring terror and awe." I looked up the Spanish. Sure enough, *"Santo y terrible es su nombre."*

Who wants to be called *terrible,* "dreadful"? And besides, only God is dreadful, that is, inspiring awe. Only God is reverend. Don't call me reverend, because I am not. No man is. Women weren't being ordained in those days, and besides, why would a nice girl like you want to be called "terrible"? *"Santo y terrible es su nombre."*

My committee work for the Presbytery took an ironic twist. I became a member, and then chairman, of the committee on Candidates and Enlistment. I, who didn't believe in ordination in my heart, took charge of the Presbytery's function of care and examination, and ordination, of new candidates. I did it with a will.

Some who offered themselves I discouraged. One of them has been eternally grateful since, and remains a close personal friend. Others I guided and challenged. I insisted that they use seminary as an opportunity to learn the Bible and the original languages, because that would be the basis of their function. I had found the phrase "teaching elder" in the polity of the Presbyterian Church. It was a way of describing the clergy that I could tolerate. There were two kinds of elders, teaching elders and ruling elders. The word

"Presbyterian" comes from the Greek work for "elder." So, ruling elders govern the church and the teaching elder, who has learned all this Greek and Hebrew and church history, will teach. Mostly he will teach what the Scripture says, and will make inferences as to what it means, perhaps, for people today. And I, as Chairman of Candidates for the Presbytery, will bend things in this direction as much as possible.

The traditional Scottish Presbyterian word for clergy was "minister." I seldom used it, because I had come to believe that *all* the Christians were called to ministry, "service," "doing for others." I wouldn't let them call *me* "the minister," for fear they might think *they* didn't have a ministry as important, or more important, than mine.

A mistranslation of a New Testament sentence was crucial. Ephesians 4:11-12 says, "And his gifts were that some should be apostles, some prophets, some evangelists, some pastors and teachers, for the equipment of the saints, for the work of the ministry, for building up the body of Christ..." "The body of Christ" is the church. The mistranslation is the insertion of a fatal comma, absolutely unjustified by the original Greek, after the word "saints." All the Christians are saints, and the sentence means "his gifts were that some should be apostles... pastors and teachers, for the equipment of the saints for the work of the ministry." It was to prepare the saints, *all* the Christians, to do the work of the ministry. The mistranslation, originally pointed out honestly enough by a seminary professor, showed that professional clergy bias—Dr. John Mackay had not hesitated to use that very phrase—has plagued the history of Christianity from the beginning. I sometimes wish I had let that warn me away from the clergy experience altogether. Did I really need to have gone through all that?

It went well for a while in the local churches I served. It was more teaching than ritual, and there were those who liked that. But there was also a longing for a priest, an official forgiver, a representative of God, a mini-substitute, who would somehow sanction in God's name whatever people were doing, including inventing atomic bombs and dropping napalm and Agent Orange on little children.

In the long run, it failed, and I can see now more clearly than ever why. The old cartoon of the guy sawing off the limb he's sitting on seems appropriate. If I don't believe, really, in what I'm doing, it's hardly any wonder that such an earnest person cannot keep on doing it indefinitely.

The General Assembly of the Presbyterian Church authorized, and mandated, a church-wide study, to be conducted in the presbyteries and in every local church, on the topic, "The Church and Its Changing Ministry." A handbook for study was written by a national committee and distributed to local churches. I was very excited about it—here were these far-out and subversive ideas, which I had thought were almost unique to me, laid right out there to challenge everyone at all levels in the entire church. The Church and Its Changing Ministry—the whole church has a ministry; the clergy, formerly called "ministers," are the ones who prepare all the members for their ministry.

We formed groups to study it in both local congregations. There were some excited people in both groups. Each church formed a Board of Deacons for the first time to coordinate and administer "outreach," which took up some of the traditional sorts of "help to the needy"—used clothing, funds for transportation to hospitals and welfare offices, that sort of thing.

I was made chairman of the Presbytery Commission on The Church and Its Changing Ministry. We were charged to study the matter in greater depth and bring proposals to a special meeting of the Synod of New Mexico, which would vote on and make recommendations to the General Assembly.

A group of us, ruling and teaching elders, prepared a lengthy list of proposals, mostly designed to share "the ministry" with the whole church and undermine the specialness of the clergy.

The first proposal, designed to clear the air—to set the mood, one could say—was a sort of proclamation *forbidding* anyone to refer henceforth to any of the teaching elders of the presbytery as "Reverend," and stating that only God was reverend and so forth. Well, the proceedings stalled right away. The official self-appointed stuffed shirts began to swell and bluster. They moved to table the motion, which was their typical tactic to ensure non-action without having to put a negative vote on record. The media caught this one, somehow, and played it up, and also ignored much more significant matters that were taken up later in that same synod meeting. Before that little flap was over, I had been interviewed for a column in the Religion section of *Time Magazine*, "What to Call the Preacher." [Nov. 30, 1962 —ed.] My answer was, "Call me Harry."

The more significant items were more serious in their design to undermine the stuffed-shirt fat-cat pastors. "All Presbyterian ministers are equal," the traditional polity declared over and over, but the Scottish church-history professor had warned us clearly, paraphrasing Orwell in *Animal Farm*, "...but some are more equal than others." We proposed parity of pension among all teaching elders. It was unfair, and un-Christian, we said, that missionaries on minimum salary should serve all those decades of active life on extremely little—while others had huge salaries and Cadillacs and insurance policies and expense accounts—and then at the end of active service, serving the Lord twenty four hours a day (was anyone doing *less*?), be further penalized by receiving a tiny pension to match the decades of tiny salary. All pension monies should be pooled and then divided equally.

The uproar was marvelous to behold. Those receiving appreciably more than minimum salary leaped to oppose. The Committee was called "Marxist." The Biblical phrase, "from each according to his ability, to each according to his need," was dismissed as un-Christian, as if Marx's quotation of Amos and Luke made the ideas *his* and not theirs!

I didn't help matters by stating, "If this upsets you, wait till you hear the next proposal." It was parity of salary. All the workers in the Lord's vineyard should get the same take-home pay. There was Biblical precedent, historical and parabolic, but both measures failed. The flap about the church and its changing ministry died down and finally went away. Fat cats were secure in their ancient superiority.

The church fended off reform. "Ministry" continued much as before, and I learned to call it "caretaker religion."

15. CARETAKER RELIGION

It must be said that I was not doing exactly what the Board of National Missions wanted done. They had not really intended to turn loose a modern-day combination of Amos and Jeremiah in the midst of the Federal atomic weapons development agencies of New Mexico. They had been totally unaware also that the word "reverend" was so pernicious. They were just trying to keep the churches open and functioning. The clue to the intent of the Presbyterian Board of National Missions was the monthly report that had to be sent to New York before the Board's share of the monthly salary would be sent back.

The monthly report was essentially a body count. How many bodies were in attendance at each weekly worship service? How many were in attendance at Sunday School? How many at midweek services, like prayer meetings, or Bible-study classes? How many pastoral calls did you make each week?

What does one count? The babe in arms that drowned out the Sunday sermon? Well, she was present! What constitutes a pastoral call? Dropping off the information to the volunteer who typed the

How God Died 63

bulletin for the weekly service? Big numbers always looked better than little ones. Small numbers required explanation in the narrative section of the report. "No one in Placitas leaves home for three days after a snowstorm." There was an almost irresistible temptation to cheat.

I came to hate the task of filling out the report, even though the numbers may have seemed encouraging to whoever read them in New York. More people *were* attending, as a matter of fact, but I could never be content with numbers. I worked hard to bring the parish to what was called "self-support," which meant we wouldn't need any more National Missions money, and I wouldn't need to fill out any more monthly reports.

This accounting was about "building up the body of Christ," as that fatal Bible verse about ministry had stated. I was fortifying the institution, what a colleague in the Philadelphia staff offices called "ecclesiasticating." I saw it as a hindrance, even an obstruction, to my prophetic function.

As I studied the Biblical message, and saw how it seemed to apply to the current local and world situation, it often felt like a choice had to be made. Do I say the truth plainly, or do I water it down so as not to offend those inventors of nuclear weapons who have come into the church one after another and finally have taken positions as ruling elders? Do I say the truth plainly, or muffle it so as to offend less these slum landlords, these transplanted racists, these jingoistic America-firsters, these know-nothings?

Pastoral calls—I was faithful in calling on the sick, the elderly, the infirm. I helped them get to the clinics. I visited and prayed with the families of the dead and dying. I found persons whom I really liked, liked to be with, liked to visit. There were some who became my personal friends, who shared a kind of search. We even called it "our quest." We shared books, introduced each other to authors, and talked and talked. Were those visits "pastoral calls"? I stopped by for beans and chile and a pork chop, almost every week, on the evening of the Bible-study class. I felt at home, felt accepted, learned to relax a little, even. Were those visits to be counted on the report as "pastoral calls"? I could tell that those folks were doing me much more good than any good I was doing them.

I began to sense a difference between the quest—the search for something that could be called Truth, something the prophets regarded as their "message" for their time, something that could now be called a "message" for our time—and religion, or ecclesiasticating.

We studied the sociology of religion. Religion is everywhere. Sometimes it becomes established, linked to the state and its monopoly on force ("the establishment"). When that happens, bad things always result, and the prophetic message has to go underground. I'd spent a year in Fascist Franco Spain and knew from firsthand experience what established religion was like. But people long for religion exactly because it represents stability and order.

The conflict between the prophetic message and religion is in the Bible. The priests of the temple, the king usually, the rabbis, the Pharisees and the Sadducees—they all represent religion, organized ecclesiastical institutions that maintain order, resist change, and keep people in their proper places. The late New Testament epistles are already doing this for the brand-new institution, the Christian Church, organizing it, keeping it "in order," ecclesiasticating. And prophets are always threatening that order, bringing in fresh radical ideas—or old neglected ones—like justice and truth.

Religion was the obstacle, it seemed to me. Later, when I could put it in mythological terms, it became clearer. Religion, popes, bishops, presbytery committees, tradition written and unwritten, ecclesiastical boards and institutions—they were all an aspect of Hold-Fast, the ogre who ate heroic troublemakers and spat out the little pieces.

The people listened to me, and some of them were challenged by the quest. Most were not. They didn't like innovation. They didn't like "relevance." They didn't want us to examine what Hosea or Jesus would say about increasing the budget for the manufacture of additional nerve gas. They wanted religion to do what it has always done. "Placate the numinous," which put more crassly means, "Get God off our backs!" Do the prayers, the rituals, the ceremonies. The Presbyterians have never been very impressive in the pageantry department, and I least of all—my costume was a white shirt, black tie, black jacket and The Book! Do the necessary hocus-pocus, mumbo-jumbo to keep God at bay.

Don't let all those haunting questions come into consciousness. Hush that Voice. "Sanctify whatever society is doing, in the name of a Higher Power." That is, sanctify what *we* are doing, assure us that everything is all right, that we are forgiven, that grace is cheap and the Way is easy. Hush about Justice. Hush about Love, *real* love. Give us sentimentality and cuteness.

I resisted that temptation, for the most part. When I didn't, there was as it were a burning fire within my bones. I was never comfortable in the role of institutional caretaker. I was never kept in line by any sense of obligation to be obedient and loyal to the institution. If anything, I was suspicious of the institution.

16. HERETIC

It is safe to state that my pre-seminary theology was "conservative." I had had my taste of fundamentalism and turned away, but I had not progressed very far. I had heard one of the Intervarsity preachers rant against Barthianism, but I didn't know what he meant. I found out in seminary, and for a while I was a Barthian myself, I suppose. The theology was also called Neo-orthodox, and the chief spokesman was Karl Barth, a Swiss

Calvinist theologian. Actually, we read less of Barth than of Emil Brunner, another Swiss of the same school.

Neo-orthodox theologians do not accept Biblical inerrancy. They are trying to reach thoughtful, reasonable people. But there is still a shrill note in their message. God is Wholly Other. God speaks, in the Bible, and man must listen. Both Barth and Brunner really pushed hard with Calvin's old theme of the Sovereignty of God. God calls sinful man back to himself. It was with this kind of theology that I went sight unseen out to New Mexico after finishing seminary.

Out in the desert, after formal schooling was finally completed, I discovered the wonder of reading—literature, history and more theology. I was strongly moved by the Liberal Social Gospel material, which had been downplayed in seminary. Princeton really was a very conservative, high-class place, and I had little business being there, given my lowly socioeconomic origins. But I only figured all that out later.

What did God have to say to poor people, to farmers, to factory workers? What were missionaries really trying to do? Save the souls of the lost, or make sure white folks get to run the whole world for their own benefit? Saving souls interested me less and less.

I found myself learning from the cultures I had been sent out to obliterate, and that undermined the obliteration process. I became less intent on trying to get people to believe what I happened to believe, partly because what I believed was in a ridiculous state of flux and I knew it.

I found the writings of Rudolph Bultmann. He gave Karl Barth a hard time from the opposite end of the spectrum from the fundamentalists. Bultmann practically accused Barth of being a fundamentalist himself! Barth asserted, "Christianity is not a religion." He meant it was simply the truth.

Bultmann chuckled, "Of course, it's a religion!" Bultmann

insisted that Barth state his presuppositions. Barth declared that he had none, that he merely stated the truth, as it was plainly put in the Bible. Bultmann chuckled more, "Everyone has his presuppositions, including you, Karl!"

Bultmann said the message from God was embedded in myth. We have to extricate that message from the myth. "Demythologization" became the new magic word. I went along with Bultmann for a while, but found myself on a greased slide. Soon I was saying "*re*mythologization," and came to believe that myth is all there is. The message *has* to be myth, it only comes in that language.

I spent the crucial summer of 1965 studying at San Francisco Theological Seminary in San Anselmo, California. It was the beginning of a doctoral program that I never finished. It was an eye-opener. I heard professors state things from the podium, things that I had been fearful of thinking. I mean, one doesn't want to be disloyal, wishy-washy, saying one thing one day and something contradictory the next. And I had been doing that. One of the professors exclaimed, "It's no wonder the church is confused. It used to take several hundred years to work our way through a theological position. Now it happens every ten years, or less!" It was certainly happening inside me with confusing rapidity.

Another professor clarified the origins of Christianity as a mystery religion. We analyzed the origins of the New Testament. There were Jewish parts that said that Jesus was a rabbi, and Gnostic parts that said that Jesus was an emanation from the Absolute. There was the mystery religion that Paul invented, and so on. I turned back to the prophets, where the message was clear enough—justice, mercy and truth—and I thought of Jesus as another prophet, murdered by those who refused his message. It had happened to earlier prophets.

Still another professor cut an important tether. "We're Calvinists by *tradition*. That's the name of the history of this branch of the church. We're not Calvinists because it's *true!*" Look out. My loyalty to The Church was dwindling at an alarming rate already. Tradition wouldn't hold me in place. I came home from that summer aware that my days were numbered in the institution. I told a friend and fellow pastor, "I'll probably demit by Christmas." Actually I lasted until the following summer.

Another school of theology, if that's the right name for it, seemed right for me. I discovered the authors while I was out in California. They were mostly young theologians, my age, who had stayed in seminaries rather than become missionaries— Altizer, Hamilton, Vahanian, Pelz. It was called the God-is-dead theology. I became the local New Mexico resource person on the fad, and lectured at the university and on local TV.

God is dead. A *New Yorker* cartoon came into my hands: A portly middle-aged gentleman in clerical collar in his sumptuous church office exclaims to the scared-looking much younger man also in clerical collar, "It's hard to imagine much of a future in the church for a young pastor who believes that God is dead!"

Bull's-eye! There is none, I found out. Actually the God-is-dead theologians puzzled me, every one of them. They seemed to think that God—the Creator of the Universe, the Origin of Power and Justice and Love in all the Cosmos—*had died*, and that we should have a funeral. Whenever someone tried to make them make sense of that, they objected.

"You mean God has experienced Death through the death of Jesus?"

"No, that's the old incarnation theory."

"You mean God is immanent in all things, and since Death is part of life, God dies every time one of his creatures dies?"

"No, that's pantheism."

"You mean the God we've been worshipping was an idol. Not God at all. Not the Living God. Dead! A dead idol?" (That's what I had come to believe and still to this day believe.)

"No. God died. We must mourn his death."

I was just finding my solution to the puzzle, that God is a metaphor, and these guys were taking God literally and seriously! And everybody in New Mexico, thanks to the media, thought I was one of them, that I agreed with them! As a school of theology, God-is-dead was very short-lived. I don't know of anyone who believes in it now.

Yet I find that I still do believe my version of it. "God" (now I need the quotation marks again) is an idol. He is the most popular idol in our culture, after Mammon, which is money. But he exists in people's heads only, or in their attempts to depict him and describe him. It is important to note that the prophets forbade attempts to name him or to depict him artistically. Recall that graven images were forbidden altogether in the Ten Commandments. The prophets' warnings went unheeded, per usual, and "God" became the greatest idol there has ever been.

I recall how this awareness awoke in me. In a study group, some of us were doubting the literal reality of hell. Would a just and loving God condemn any of his creatures, for any reason, to eternal conscious torment? Some of the reasons that had been suggested for such condemnation were very arbitrary. Failure to hear the message of the Good News, failure to heed the message, even though it was delivered by extremely unloving persons—these failures and refusals could result in an eternity in hell, some seemed to be saying. I didn't believe it, and some of those in the group didn't believe it either:

"God loves us all. He loves all people. If there is only one God, he has to be everybody's, and other ways of approaching him and understanding him are as good as ours."

"The 'God' of the Christians can be exposed as an idol, whenever we see him separating a group from the whole, making one portion of the whole better than the rest."

One lady in the group objected. "If there is no hell, why be good?"

We never convinced her, but it clarified things for some of us. If we're "being good," or "doing good," in order to avoid being sent to hell by a vengeful, punishing God, that's a very childish way to live. Some of us turned the same idea back on "God"—what kind of God is this? Why would anyone want to worship and love and obey him? He is utterly unadmirable. He reminds me of a bad king, a bad general, a bad father—mean, ready to abuse his power and authority, an idol of cruelty, like Moloch of the Moabites. And when God-is-dead came along, I was able to say, *"That's* the God who died. That idol died. That idol never lived at all."

That idol never had any reality, except in the minds of the mean-hearted people who invented him. It did not correspond to anything that really existed. That male, patriarchal, cruel, warmongering, arbitrary potentate, who supposedly made and rules the Cosmos, isn't there. The idol did not speak, did not refute our logic and our prayers.

We went through a test, like that of the prophet Elijah on Mt. Carmel. We demanded that God clarify this, just as Elijah had demanded. "The God who answers by fire, he is God!" We prayed. We waited. We even teased a little, as Elijah had teased the prophets of Baal. "Cry aloud! For he is a God. Either he is musing, or he has gone aside, or he is on a journey, or perhaps he is asleep and must be awakened." But there was no voice; no one answered, no one heeded.

God died. That idol "God" died. Since then I have concluded that this test is going on all the time. The fact that "God" allows Jerry Falwell, Pat Robertson, Oral Roberts, Jimmy Swaggart and Oliver North to speak for him to millions of people eager to be swayed and swindled, while they themselves display the most blatantly unethical, anti-humane behavior, is the proof Thomas Aquinas labored so hard for. Proof of the existence of God—in reverse! There is no such God. If he existed, he would zap these false prophets, rid the earth of their lies and crimes, clear the air, and clean the record. The fact that he doesn't proves that he doesn't exist at all.

Before I found the God-is-dead stuff, I found Bishop Robinson's book, *Honest to God*. It was an elementary analysis of the doctrine of God, and the most surprising thing about it was that an Anglican bishop wrote it. The honesty was remarkable, from a position so high in the ecclesiastical organization. He admitted that his thinking was more modern than the traditional theological formulae.

In the three-story universe of Biblical times, God was "up there," in Heaven. In the modern Copernican world of solar systems and galaxies, God was "out there," in what C.S. Lewis still called "Deep Heaven" in his sci-fi allegories, *Out of the Silent Planet* and *Perelandra*. Robinson said God was neither up there nor out there. He seemed to be trying to popularize Paul Tillich's idea of God as the Ground of Our Being, a basically Hindu idea. I liked it, and tried it, but for me, then, as my world was collapsing, "There was no voice. No one answered. No one heeded." God was not up there, nor was he out there, nor was he, as far as I could tell at the time, "in there." I concluded that an idol of mine had died.

So, in the last stages before I left the organized ecclesiastical institution, I was perfectly aware of my heresy, and called myself out. I preached a sermon called "Confessions of an Atheist," in which I suggested that Marx, Nietzsche and Freud were more true to the message of the prophets, because of their ruthless honesty, than many who glibly mouthed the name "God." I studied in detail the impressive list of heresies condemned by the official churches, both Catholic and Protestant. I found that I agreed with the heretics in almost all cases. At the very least I agreed with their right to interpret for themselves both the texts and their direct experiences of that Something, which they still called "God" and I no longer could.

I resented what Erich Fromm had taught me to call "irrational authority." Rational authority, in contrast, is legitimate, based on knowledge. If you don't know how to cane a chair, and want to learn how, you can come to me and ask, and if I'm able and inclined, I'll be your authority on chair caning, because I *do* know how. My authority over you lasts as long as I continue to know more about it than you. It is nothing personal at all, it is based on who knows what.

Irrational authority is based on rank and power. Power can be physical or psychological. Irrational authority is used by parents, police, armies, most teachers, bishops, popes, inquisitions, bosses, chairpersons of faculty committees. "Do it because I say so." "Believe it because I say so." I find that last command about beliefs especially reprehensible—belief based on irrational authority is *disbelief*, laziness, inattention, fear, and a sort of deliberately self-imposed stupidity. Believe it because you've studied it and are convinced it's true! Don't believe anything much or quickly.

Irrational authority cost the heretics dearly. I am grateful that I live in this era of disbelief, in which inquisitions lack the power and authority to flat out kill the likes of me. I would not have lasted long in the Spain of Felipe II, or the Geneva of John Calvin, or the Massachusetts Bay Colony of Cotton Mather. Hopefully, I could have fled to William Penn's Holy Experiment, although I would probably have ended up disappointed in that, too.

I was a heretic for a while. The structure of belief eroded away gradually. Early on, I didn't believe in hell or the Virgin Birth. Later, I questioned the justice of the Penal-Substitutionary theory of the atonement. How could a just judge deliberately punish the wrong person? What kind of justice is that? If Jesus took my place, took the rap for me, how am I improved? You mean I just "get off," like these crooks who are patently, obviously immoral and chatter away about how forgiven they are? No, thanks.

I questioned the whole idea of salvation, as used by some, if not most. "Are you saved?" they ask. You can get rid of them by saying, "Yes," meaning that you believe that Jesus died in your place for your sins on the cross, so that you can get off without punishment. You'll never get rid of them if you go on about collective guilt or paying taxes to pay for immoral wars, or if you start in on our inherent mortality, which no "sacrifice" can take away.

I rejected the authority of the church. In the case of popes it was easy, since I wasn't personally involved and the history was plain. The history of presbyteries was closer to home and harder to find, but ultimately just as convincing. That vote wasn't "God" deciding, it was the rule of the majority of a group of narrow-minded, self-seeking ordinary sinful human beings. A Scottish novel by John Buchan, *Witchwood*, contains a priceless line in which an elderly Scottish lady analyzes the presbytery: "a kind o' Papery, wi' fifty papes, instead o' ane." I had dealt with three different local sessions in my career—the ruling elders ruled, not because of any superior knowledge or morality. They were afraid to wield the irrational authority they had been given and usually declined to use it—they thought and behaved like human politicians.

The whole church enterprise began to look phoney to me. The clergy were seeking soft positions with lots of money and little effort. The laity wanted comfort more than anything else.

17. SOCIAL ACTION

I was thinking my way out of the ecclesiastical organization, and at the same time my activities in the real world were becoming decisive. The church itself had a Department of Social Education and Action, at local, synod and national levels. These were the "activists," those who wanted the church's message to make a difference in the world, who were as concerned about social justice as about the saving of souls.

During the study of The Church and Its Changing Ministry I found the concept of pastor as coach of an athletic team. "For the preparation of the saints for the work of the ministry..." The lay people have the ministry; *they* have to play the game; I'm the coach. Almost immediately I moved to the concept of the player-coach. I couldn't stay on the sidelines, instructing and calling plays, yelling and throwing my hat down and stomping on it—I jumped in and made tackles myself.

A basic question was at stake. If the gospel is true, what is implied for human society? I became involved gradually in the Black Liberation Movement. I became really committed to the notion of equality, and found it in the church's message to the world, clearer than in the theoretical writings of Thomas Jefferson, who owned slaves. We are all sinners. God loves us all. He forgives us all. He calls us all to love one another and even to love our enemies. I didn't make any of that up.

I joined the local NAACP. There were very few blacks in Albuquerque, but I joined their cause. I also tried to make a big thing out of the racial and ethnic mixture of people who made up the congregation of one of the churches I served as pastor. Besides gringos, we had chicanos, although not all of them liked that word for themselves—descendants of the Spanish-speaking people who were already here when the territory was taken from Mexico in 1846. We also had natives of the western hemisphere, who are not from India! We had to deal with some language barriers, especially among the elderly.

I helped picket apartment complexes that were caught refusing to rent to blacks. I regarded Martin Luther King as the prophet of our time, and I challenged the church, local and national, to accept his movement as a way to let Christianity have an influence on human life. It was an early form of what is now called Liberation Theology. Christians were challenged to leave off racial oppression, to quit it, in the name of their own faith, and King challenged the oppressed to quit allowing it, quit giving in to it, in the name of the very same faith.

I went to Selma in March of 1965 as part of the March on Montgomery. Several of the candidates under the care of the presbytery, whom I was supervising, organized a busload of students from the seminary in San Francisco to take part in the march. One called me, and was delighted when I said, "Pick me up on your way through Albuquerque." I was the only Chairman of Candidates on the bus—most of the students had what they called "old fogeys" to deal with as chairmen.

Several seminary professors of church history, including those from California and Pittsburgh, met in Selma. Somehow that seemed significant to me. The historians sensed history being made and wanted to be in on it.

The week's experience affected me deeply. Part of the inner reaction that I hadn't expected was my growing difficulty with the clerical role. When some of the students whipped out clerical collars for the last day's march through the streets of Montgomery, Alabama, I was stunned. I had been called a roustabout by reporters all week. Our task was to take down and put up huge circus tents for the 300 marchers who actually walked all the way from Selma to Montgomery; it was hard work. I felt myself more at home with "roustabout," sledge hammer at the ready, than "reverend." I never once wore a clerical collar. The most I could manage in my entire career was a black robe, used only at ordinations of other people, and I hated it.

When I came home from Selma, I was made Chairman of the Commission on Race of the Presbytery. I do not believe that Commission accomplished anything, except to give a few of us the illusion that the church was involved in the struggle. The large prestigious churches of the presbytery, what I and others came to call "the fat-cat churches," used all their influence the other way, to hinder integration and to continue to keep dark-skinned people in their subservient place.

I wrote a thesis while at seminary in San Anselmo. We read the ponderous two-volume work by Ernst Troeltsch (rhymes with "belch") called *The Social Teachings of the Christian Churches and Groups*. It was all of church history from the point of view of "social action." In it Troeltsch makes clear that Christianity has been relevant to the socioeconomic and political realities of human existence only twice. Mostly it is irrelevant, saving souls for heaven and having no impact at all on earth.

But twice it was relevant. First, during the period of massive monolithic Roman Catholic unity and control in the High Middle Ages in Europe, when the pope and his clergy named kings and emperors to their subservient positions, and all of daily life was regulated by the unchallenged power of the church. Second, during the rise of capitalism, when Calvinist teaching about work, savings and worldly signs of heavenly grace permeated the rise and spread of the new system of economic production and distribution.

I proposed that in Martin Luther King, Christianity had a third chance to be relevant to what humans were doing. A worldwide revolution was in progress, in which non-European people were throwing off the colonialist oppression of the Europeans. The revolution was completed in China and India, under way and unstoppable in Africa and Southeast Asia, in spite of the military efforts of the USA. The revolution was just getting started in Latin America.

Part of that revolution was taking place inside the USA, in the uprising of the former slaves, non-Europeans who had their roots in Africa. In Martin Luther King, Christianity touched that revolution. My thesis laid out how relevant Christianity could once again become by allowing that revolution to take place nonviolently, thus minimizing the level of revenge and recrimination that otherwise accompanies social upheaval. I

How God Died

thought it was a brilliant paper, but the church ignored it, just as it was ignoring King himself. The process affected me, but not the church, nor the revolution.

Opponents in the fat-cat churches inquired, "That Willson—is he black?" I am not. I spent just enough time working in Martin Luther King's organization in Atlanta, the entire long hot summer of 1967, to catch myself a time or two thinking black, a little. But that was already after I was gone from the church. No, my test was whether the church was going to support the blacks' demand for liberation and equality, or not—and the decision was clearly, "No, we're not. The church will remain on the side of the white status quo."

The other main thrust of my involvement in social action was my opposition to the war in Vietnam. I recall throwing a copy of *Time Magazine* against the wall in the dormitory room at Lafayette College in 1952, shouting, "We're on the wrong side!" Ho Chi Minh represented the Vietnamese people's intent to get European colonialists *out*. He had been repudiated at the Versailles Conference of 1919 by Woodrow Wilson—"self-determination of peoples" was not intended to include "colored people." The fact that Ho became a Marxist, and did find encouragement from Lenin and the Soviet Union, didn't change that he really was part of that same World Revolution and determined to throw European invaders out of Indochina.

The revolutionaries succeeded in 1954, at Dien Bien Phu, but the Americans leaped in and, in spite of de Gaulle's warnings, replaced the French as conquerors. The war of aggression, even though couched in terms of the need to contain Communism, was blatantly immoral, illegal and unconstitutional, and served no perceptible American self-interest—except those of the suppliers of military materials, like body bags. American involvement prolonged the Vietnamese war of liberation for nineteen bloody years.

I did not see how the churches, or individual Christians, could possibly approve of that war, and I said so, in season and out of season, from the pulpit, in the newspapers and at every opportunity, often in the streets. I counseled draft-age students. "Once you decide you're not going, we can do this and this and this. You must decide it, and state it to me flatly and emphatically. Then we can proceed."

I found that while not all Christians liked the war exactly, they did not see it as antithetical to their Christian beliefs. The rank and file were content to let the government and its experts be in charge of that department and didn't want to think about it. Hearers of my preaching called into question my loyalty, and they were right to do so. A parishioner asked me at the door of the church, "Do you really mean to say that you understand the history of Southeast Asia and our policy there better than the Secretary of State of the United States?"

"Lord, yes!" I exclaimed instantly. "Yes! Yes!" It was taken as arrogance on my part.

I was preaching an Advent sermon series called "Peace on Earth." The head pastor of the downtown fat-cat church caught wind of it and likened me, in a published sermon of his own, to those referred to by the prophet Jeremiah: "They cry, 'Peace, peace,' when there is no peace."

I had studied Jeremiah more than he had. Jeremiah was that disloyal prophet of the besieged and doomed Kingdom of Judah, who warned the people and the king that God had changed sides, because of justice questions. In the comment about peace, Jeremiah was referring to the priests and fat-cat *false* prophets of the king and the establishment, who said not to worry about Nebuchadnezzar—there would be "peace, peace"—whereas Jeremiah knew that there would not.

I became more shrill. "Chickens will come home to roost." "Truth and Justice will out in the long run." "Followers of Christ will not be spared the pending trouble." It was then that the mother of the marine, who was throwing Agent Orange on the Vietnamese people, told me she wanted comfort, not truth, not the message of prophets, old or new. It didn't work. "Americans had better be hoping that there is *not* a just God!" I preached.

I began to write "poetry." Some of it was a little harsh.

> "Life is cheap there."
> So we defend the slaughter
> Burning and bombing villages
> Full of children
> Starving whole populations
> Shooting anything that moves.
>
> "Life is cheap there."
> As though you had to attend
> an American Sunday School
> in order to learn
> to love your babies, your wives,
> your friends and neighbors.

At a called meeting of the presbytery, I asked to make an announcement. My announcement was to read the essence of a petition, put out by S.A.N.E., a nationally known activist group, calling for a cessation of the indiscriminate bombing of North Vietnam and an opening of negotiations with the People's National Liberation Front, which the American high command called "the Viet Cong."

The other fat-cat pastor, in whose huge fancy sanctuary we were meeting, leaped up and demanded equal time, even though it was a called meeting. I said I wasn't asking for action—I was inviting other members of the presbytery to sign the petition, as individuals, after the meeting. He demanded the right to refute the content of the petition, since it was Communist inspired and at best of no concern to Christians.

I said that Communism had little or nothing to do with it, and burst out, "Jesus would not approve of our throwing bombs on little children!"

He was utterly nonplussed. "Oh," he stated, in an infuriatingly smug and oleaginous manner, "I can imagine a situation in which Jesus would approve of throwing bombs on little children."

I was dumbstruck. I'm sure I had paled seriously when I finally gasped, very quietly, "We're not talking about the same Jesus." It was at that moment that I left the church, although it took six months for the externals to fall into place. At that moment, I knew I was out.

Two men and I, out of forty present, signed the petition. I could find very little companionship inside the church. I thought I understood the message of the church, but evidently I did not. I began to see the church as a propaganda agency for the Pentagon, an idea which was slightly overblown, to be sure, but not much. Mine was the perspective of an embattled, and losing, heretic. In the end I had to separate myself from that organization, especially from that particular bomb-throwing pastor, the most powerful and most highly regarded in the entire Synod of New Mexico. "All Presbyterian ministers are equal, but some are more equal than others." Money, prestige, position—all counted for more than "equality." His session and congregation were full of generals and colonels from the local air base, and engineers and section supervisors from the local atomic weapons laboratory.

It was Advent, 1965. I continued the sermon series entitled, "Peace on Earth." The sermons were not snowy medieval Christmas cards. They were sharp challenges, and not appreciated. I lasted until June, 1966, and then resigned.

18. DEMISSION

The treasury of the Alameda Presbyterian Church was empty. There was no money to pay the next month's salary, which was the lion's share of the budget. It was a textbook case of how money talks. When enough people are through supporting the local church and its "mission," to the point of refusing to put anything more into the offering plate, things go into motion. I offered to resign, and the Session accepted the resignation.

This family crisis was far less urgent. My wife had finished her degree in education at the university and had a contract to teach in the Albuquerque Public Schools in the fall. But it was a personal crisis, for me. Now what do I do? Through the urging and recommendation of Adela, my fellow quester in Placitas, I found a very odd-shaped slot on the faculty of Albuquerque Academy, a private boys' preparatory school, which her two boys had been attending for several years. I taught science, math, history and English to sixth graders. The fact that I was bilingual and could have taught Spanish also, if needed, seemed to be the qualification that impressed the headmaster most.

I loved teaching, loved the boys. They liked me. They said they liked the way I laughed. They liked the way I listened to what *they* had to say. We learned much together. To me it felt like a kind of ministry, the kind I used to pretend I was preparing others for—I had finally found my own.

I stayed on as Temporary Supply Pastor in Placitas, preaching on Sundays, visiting, conducting mid-week study groups. But it felt more and more dishonest. I didn't believe enough of it anymore. Many of the hymns were impossible for me to sing. The Lord's Prayer was hollow. The prayer of confession was insincere and deleterious in its effect. The Apostles Creed was a sham, a mockery. As Christmas loomed I resigned altogether. I had found my ministry, and it wasn't conducting worship services in a false manner; it was teaching.

Ironies abound in life. A year earlier, one month after I could find only two additional signatures for that S.A.N.E. petition, the presbytery elected me moderator. The function of the moderator was to chair meetings in a formal manner, following Roberts Rules of Order. The office carried no real power or authority, except as one could influence debate by insisting, more or less, on order. But it was an honor—and I was frankly puzzled that it had been bestowed on me, especially at that particular time. The irony was that I had to relinquish the chair to the vice-moderator at several key moments during that year in which I served: First, my resignation from the Alameda church; then my resignation from Placitas; and finally, my own petition "to demit the ministry."

I had used the phrase, only partly in jest, upon my return from that summer at the seminary in San Anselmo, California. Now, during that first fall of my teaching experience, a strange movement arose in the church, perhaps a backlash against all that "foolishness" that had been aired during the study of The Church and Its Changing Ministry. The Ministerial Relations Committee decided to go after those members of the presbytery who were not serving churches as pastors. There always are some. Some are bureaucrats in the system of synod and national boards. Some are missionaries abroad. Some are officially retired. But some have no clear ecclesiastical connection or function. I was about to become one of them, and if ever asked I was ready to declare that my ministry was teaching history and English and math and science to sixth grade boys. But the committee was "coming after" the likes of me. It helped me decide to petition to demit.

"Demit" means "to send away." The laws of the Presbyterian Church allowed ordained persons to be unordained, in effect, without trial, by petitioning for such action. There was a one-year waiting period to be used for counseling the petitioner before the

How God Died

new status went into effect following a second vote by the presbytery. During the final meeting of the presbytery over which I presided as moderator, I relinquished the chair to the vice-moderator and presented my petition to demit. That evening, during formal official worship services, I conducted the Sacrament of the Lord's Supper for the last time, functioning as moderator. I preached my last sermon, "The Irony of Presbyterian Ecclesiastical History," a sort of parody of an important book by Reinholdt Niebuhr, called *The Irony of American History*. I traced the relation of the Christian Church to war from before Constantine to Vietnam. The Presbyterian Church has always been very proud of its active role in the American Revolutionary War. George III called the conflict, "that Presbyterian rebellion." The Presbyterian Church split in two over the Civil War and slavery. The Presbyterian Church supported all U.S. wars, and supported the one in Vietnam. I maintained that my reading of Scripture led me to conclude that the Quakers and the Mennonites were right about war, and that the Presbyterians have been wrong. I asked to demit, to be "sent away." I petitioned for an end to mission. During that year, supposedly set up for counseling, no one came looking for that lost black sheep, that scapegoat sent out into the wilderness to bear the sins of the people. Part of me wondered why no one came to try to talk me out of it. But most of me rejoiced that they were going to leave me alone; they were going to let me do what I needed to do—separate, come out, find my own way. And so it happened. I thought, "Now I'll be a loner forever." "To thine own self be true..." made more sense than ever.

I wasn't present when the presbytery voted the second time. I received by mail a copy of the proceedings. The terms of demission were very interesting. I mean the words used. It amounted to a proclamation, as follows: "The Presbytery of Rio Grande declares that the Presbytery of Newton did err in the ordination of Harry G. Willson to the ministry of the United Presbyterian Church, etc.,

etc." The rest of it directed the Stated Clerk to remove my name from the roll of the presbytery.

Included was a letter, asking which local congregation I wanted my membership transferred to, but I never answered, and never heard more. I had come to have a great deal of trouble being a pastor, that is, a shepherd. I certainly wasn't about to go back to being a sheep.

PART II

♦

PROPHET WITH NO GOD

19. THE OFFICE

"Gosh, I'm glad I'm not an archbishop!" I actually said that the other day. I'm glad I'm not a priest, not a pastor with sheep to tend, not a moderator of a presbytery or a synod or a general assembly, not a clergyman, not a reverend.

Ecclesiastical institutions are in trouble in New Mexico these days. The mainstream Protestant churches, of which I was a standard-bearer so long ago, have drifted further and further into irrelevancy. And the largest and most powerful of all the churches here, the Roman Catholic, is in serious trouble.

Several priests have been found guilty of pedophilia, sexually abusing children, especially altar boys. One lawyer gathered together a group of victims, more than twenty, and sued the Archdiocese of Santa Fe. Evidently the archbishop knew of the propensity of these priests to abuse children, but nevertheless assigned them to parishes containing children. Also, the archbishop moved slowly in response to the first lawsuits, trying to minimize publicity. Denial and cover-up was the order of the day. Concern for the reputation of the institution and its representatives outranked concern for truth or compassion for victims. The newspapers began to carry stories about pedophiliac priests and the lawsuits on behalf of the victims.

The bombshell, which perhaps explained the strange previous non-action of the archdiocese, exploded on national network television. Five women came forward, three on camera, stating that they had been seduced by the archbishop himself, while he *was* archbishop and they were fifteen to seventeen years old. Their stories appeared in the newspapers. The archbishop was out of the state, "on retreat," and has been ever since. He wrote, asking for forgiveness, without admitting that he had done any of what the women alleged. He then resigned. Three weeks later the Pope accepted his resignation, and assigned the Bishop of Lubbock to oversee the diocese. He has since been named archbishop.

Stories from the women kept coming out, and they clarified what had happened. The archbishop had instructed them to use The Pill. He and his underlings have been telling housewives with eight children that they will suffer eternal conscious torment if they use The Pill, or any effective means of contraception, but his victims are instructed to use it. What? Is he instructing them to risk hell-fire in order to protect himself?

One of the girls asked him, while he was fondling her in the home chapel her parents had built in his honor, "What if I tell on us?"

He replied, "They won't believe you. I'm the archbishop." The girl's father told that story to a newspaper reporter. The story made clear that the archbishop was not caught in the velvet grip of Aphrodite; he was exercising power—naked "spiritual" power.

Mike Wallace interviewed the three young women on television. "So, he took your virginity," he said to one.

"That's not all he took," she replied. "Within days of the time he terminated our relationship, I lost my faith."

Lost her faith. I have had to think about that phrase a great deal. That young lady lost her faith, because she believed that a man had been vested with supernatural powers, and then he used those powers to overwhelm her. Then what? She ceased to believe in those superhuman powers? What, then? She no longer believes that the Bishop of Rome is the infallible Vicar of Christ on earth, or that

Prophet With No God

all the other bishops are anything but mere men, dressed as women some of the time, pretending to be what they cannot be? She no longer believes in the Roman Catholic Church as the only vehicle of salvation? She no longer believes in salvation? She no longer believes in Christ as Savior? She no longer believes in God? What faith has she lost? I wrote to her, telling her that I lost my faith once, too, and offering to share, but she didn't reply, and I'm in no way surprised.

Many conversations are now occurring in New Mexico about abuse, child abuse, the abuse of privilege and the stupidity of enforced celibacy for priests. The new archbishop has been concerned mostly about money, which is needed to pay compensation ordered by courts and judges. He's worried that the archdiocese may go bankrupt, and that seems to trouble him more than anything deeper, like human suffering or human nature, or his church's official doctrine about sin and sex.

It could become a chance to talk about the office itself, but probably will not. It comes up in many private conversations. I hear more and more the phrase "spiritual abuse," and when I hear it, I feel touched personally. The spiritual abuse of children—yes, I suffered that. "They take away your soul," one told me. Yes, I agree. I remember!

When you're young, you are open to the influence of what could be called The Unseen. You are a natural animist—everything is alive. You can have conversations with toys, trees, birds, pet animals, clouds, spirits of all sorts, elves, leprechauns and all that. You can believe in Santa Claus and the Easter Bunny and the Tooth Fairy and Tinkerbelle and mermaids and angels and God.

In my own case, there was little magic in childhood. It was all funneled into belief in "God," which was that accusing Voice. I am closer to believing in angels and nature-spirits now than I ever was as a child. The fear of the accusing "God" who must be obeyed spoiled all the joy and spontaneity that's supposed to be typical of childhood. That feels like a kind of spiritual abuse, now. The adults around seemed so afraid of the possibility of disobedience that there was little room for fun, or play or experimentation or even curiosity. All that, in my life, has come as a mature and free adult. It was not there in childhood.

I was not abused physically by anyone, that is, sexually. I was spanked plenty, but never with a weapon, like a stick or a belt. I was strongly commanded not to fight, which was how young boys sorted things out and solved problems and arranged the pecking order. So, by refusing to fight, I remained at the bottom of the order. There was one incident, the great disobeying exception to all the rest of childhood, when provocation overcame the fear of disobedience and punishment. The pent-up rage created a dangerously invincible fighter, it turned out, but it did not feel like a triumph. I scared myself. It was the one overt indication to me that I was not having a happy childhood, and I repressed it immediately and for decades.

I was not a victim of pedophilia. I was kept in sexual ignorance longer than I wanted to be, but that did me no harm. The clergymen I knew as a child and adolescent were not harmful to me. One was a charmer of the females, and he broke one heart that I know of by marrying a war widow instead of *her*. One was a hateful and vindictive person, a fundamentalist and a liar. One was a friendly koala-bear type, totally wholesome.

I wonder what kind of clergyman I was. Too serious, too much into the issues of the day—racism, war, dishonest politicians, nuclear fallout. The youth liked me, as I recall, perhaps because I was challenging the values of their parents and they sensed an ally.

When I became a teacher, the students let me know that they were grateful that I was on their side. I received many astonishing confidences, and the administration resented my consistent refusal to pass them on.

I saw the role of teacher as temporary, based on rational

authority. As long as I knew more than they did, the authority was legitimate. We all knew that many of them would pass me, and they have, and I do not resent that in any way. We all found it liberating when I answered a question one day with the reply, "I don't know. It beats hell outa me."

The role of clergyman, however, is a different matter, especially if it's being taken seriously by anyone. I could never do it. I always knew better. Most of the people wanted a priest, some kind of special channel to God. But I felt called to be a prophet. There was this message, which had to do with justice and peace and equality. It didn't have to do with me, or my office in the church. It hardly had to do with church at all, I came to believe. I find the churches, even now, not much interested in their own message. Mostly it's building funds and yellow ribbons, supporting mass slaughter somewhere.

There are some remarkable exceptions, and I salute them. There is a hospice movement and a facility connected to an Episcopal church here in town. The churches feed the homeless, since the government cannot afford to, what with that $350 billion war budget. There is even a peace movement in the churches, which there wasn't in 1966.

But the role of clergyman, I'm convinced, is designed to set up abuse, and constitutes abuse. If no one else is being abused, the clergyman is. The great irony about all the clamor to end mandatory clerical celibacy in the Roman Catholic Church, in hopes that clerical marriage will minimize pedophilia committed *by* clergy is this: The only role *more* abusive to the one playing it than that of clergyman is that of clergyman's wife! I've come to believe that the office, the role of clergyman itself, is impossible, wed or unwed, and needs to be abolished.

No one can represent God to anyone else. Or perhaps anyone can. A bird can. No one can handle being set aside to do that "professionally." It is preposterous, and some form of abuse becomes inevitable. I was abusing myself, and my family, for as long as I allowed myself to remain in that role. It began in falsehood, and freedom and truth came to the surface only when it ended.

To pretend that someone knows better than you do who you are and what your life should consist of and what you ought to do is abuse, spiritual abuse. *You* must discover that. The best counselor in the world will simply help you do that. If he *tells* you, and especially if he tells you in the name of the Source Of All Justice And Love In All The Cosmos, he's a fraud. Why would It tell *him* what It needs to tell *you*? "If you meet the Buddha on the road, kill him." Really! And don't let him touch your sons or daughters. Teach them to think all this through for themselves and to grow up free and undeceived.

For a while some of us young pastors, all of whom were having a hard time with the role, referred to ourselves ironically as "paid lovers of people." It had a bitter ring to it, since we were paid so precious little. We were missionaries on minimum salary, depending on charity to a degree that was degrading and infuriating.

Why were we being paid anything at all—that is, to do what? To preach, to preach the gospel, but the people didn't seem to want to hear that clearly. "Stick to the gospel," which we often heard, meant, "Now you're trying again to relate that message to what is really going on in the world. Quit that!" We were paid to lead worship services. I was never sure that they accomplished anything at all. Prayers of confession that no one believed or related to themselves, prayers of petition that accomplished little, like a weekly letter to Santa Claus, to what effect? Sing hymns, read the Bible.

What else were they paying us to do? Visit the sick, comfort the dying with strange mythical assurances, visit the bereaved, bury the dead, marry some, baptize others, counsel the troubled. Spend your life minding other people's business.

A colleague found a fresh definition of a prostitute. "She does for money what she should do for love." Aha! Somehow it added to the sense that I was in an office that degraded me, and spoiled love.

It is strange how the daily news funnels itself into this enquiry. In the 1990s, the government burned down the compound of an extremist religious cult, burning to death several dozen people, including children under ten years of age. The television images were graphic, but much of the commentary was inane. To call the leader, "The Wacko from Waco," was unhelpful.

People wonder how adults could turn their lives over to a person who was certifiably mentally ill. Men gave their wives to him and women gave themselves to him—in exchange for what? Well, in exchange for certainty, it seems. Certainty is marvelous stuff, and people who have it will do strange things to keep it.

Sometimes we can admire that kind of certainty. "Give me liberty or give me death!" "I regret that I have only one life to give for my country." "Death before dishonor!" "¡Tierra o Muerte!" "Land or Death"—the outcry still seen on billboards in northern New Mexico, trying to keep alive the Spanish Land Grant recovery movement. "¡Más vale morir a pie que vivir a rodillas!"—from the Mexican Revolution and the Spanish Civil War, "It is better to die on your feet than to live on your knees."

Certainty in religious matters, these days in this country, is almost always regarded as fanaticism, and when more than one person shares the same certainty, it is quickly labeled a cult. In our time and place, you're supposed to be lukewarm about such things. In fact, nowadays the word isn't lukewarm—it's "cool." You're supposed to be *not* certain.

Our culture doesn't like people who are sure. Even though she said she envied it, my sister resented my certainty about Eliot Abrams and the Somocista "contras" in Nicaragua and the murdering of nurses and agricultural co-op personnel, all illegally funded by our tax money—because once you are certain you must be outraged. Some family members here, who worked all of their adult lives in the local nuclear weapons laboratory, resent my clarity of thought and word regarding the morality of nuclear weapons.

When the Jonestown mass suicide occurred in South America in 1978, I had an inner personal reaction similar to the one I feel today. I think I could have been a James Jones, or a David Koresh. It was a close call. My failure in the church business all those decades ago saved me from that.

The failure was caused partly by the fact that in the local churches that I was serving as pastor, I had a cult-like belief and commitment, and no one else did. I had arrived with that attitude of extreme earnestness, and was constantly frustrated by the lower level of commitment of the people in the churches. They were being very sensible. They hadn't joined a cult at all. They had joined a church, or had been born into it somehow. It was a compartment in their lives, not a total commitment. I could never turn it into a cult because that kind of commitment wasn't there. And now I'm very grateful that such was the case.

Also, I was saved by my awareness of the inherent meanness in fundamentalism. I really didn't want to be a mean person. When I caught my commitment making me mean, making the sermons shrill, making the obedience I had demonstrated look smug, I was brought up short. And I never became committed to the apocalyptic, eschatological stuff, which becomes so dangerous when taken literally. I knew very early on that all that was myth—the Last Judgement, the End of the World, the Last Battle of Armageddon—all of that is *myth*. It has to do with Antiochus Epiphanes, and with the fall of Jerusalem, and with the then pending collapse of the Roman Empire. To be sure, there may be some insight, some relevance to the current pending collapse of the

American Empire and the danger of total plutonium poisoning and global warming, but it is not to be taken personally and literally as stated in ancient texts. I knew all that early on.

I was quite a fanatic, nevertheless. A person who has never been troubled or burdened by a belief in a God who can take over your life could look at what I did in 1958 and decide that it differed only in degree from Branch Davidians of the same era moving their families to Waco. I put a wife and three children, two of them in bottles and diapers, into a little car and drove two thousand miles to a place I had never seen to take on the job of missionary pastor to three little churches, with a guaranteed income of $400 per month. It was crazy. Only a fanatic would do it. It was admired, rather than thought of as foolish and dangerous, because that kind of craziness, or at least the words to justify it, had been institutionalized in the United Presbyterian Church.

I was saved from the cult business also by my commitment to the Hebrew prophets. Not as isolated texts to be used out of context to justify whatever madness came into my head. No, I had studied them very carefully, knew them as persons, distinguished one from another, admired their moments of honest doubt. Those things are in the texts, too, along with the other statements of faith and courage. I felt like one of them, and they were *not* cult leaders. They were loners, committed to a message of justice, but not trying to organize a cult following around their own personalities. It was never really an option, or much of a danger, in my case. In fact, I was more likely to succumb to the Elijah Complex, believing wrongly that "I alone am left, a servant of the Lord God."

Twice during that crucial year of 1966, in the midst of which I resigned from the churches, I took part in what was called "the Marathon." It was a psychotherapy experience, a special sort of group therapy, in which about fifteen people stayed together "in honest meeting," nonstop, for forty-eight hours. If you wanted to participate, at two in the morning, by falling asleep, go ahead, but the group encounter went on with no let-up. The concept was originated by Fritz Perls, and brought to Albuquerque by one of his students.

I was in the very first Marathon, and then another, and they did me much good, helping me recognize and clarify feelings, and make decisions. I remember one of the key questions was, "What do you want to do when you grow up, Harry?" Another insight was, "It's OK for you to be angry with your father, Harry, but don't take it out on us. You take charge of your life."

I was very grateful for the liberating effect of the Marathon. Several more were conducted in Albuquerque. Then there was a kind of reunion of all Marathon participants at the home of the leader/therapist. I was impressed with the sort of adulation of the leader that I spotted in many of the persons attending. They were forming a sort of in-group, in which persons who had attended a Marathon were *in,* and all the rest of the population of the globe were in some sense *out.*

A moment came when the group turned to me for whatever it was that I was thinking. I was frank. "I am a little perplexed," I said. "Here we are, like the Original Twelve Apostles. Here is the Messiah of the world—" I gestured toward the leader. "What are you wanting to do? It feels like the early stages of The New Testament. I have to say to you all, 'No, thanks. I tried that. I have just liberated myself from that. I couldn't go back to that.'" The leader was offended, and so were many others. I found myself no longer a part of the Marathon Movement.

So, the cult business was a close call for me, only in a strange kind of way. I was protected from the gross insanity required to be the leader, from fire and poison and death and the responsibility for the deaths of others, by—what? It's hard to say, hard for me to say, but I am grateful, to—whatever. And I am grateful for a kind of clearheadedness and comprehension that came to me in time.

I am especially grateful for the human connections I now have that keep me from a kind of extremism, a dangerous kind of passion that is still there inside me. It's strange. How often I look at Adela and ponder our relationship and think to myself, "If it weren't for her, I'd be a bomb-throwing anarchist, dangerous to myself and others." I do not believe that passion and caring a lot and clarity and even certainty are bad things. But in my own life I find them balanced by human connections and an awareness that if I gave free rein to my craziness, people whom I care about very much and who care about me more than I can comprehend would be hurt. So I cool it.

20. RESIDUE

I dreamed that I was a contestant on a TV quiz show and was asked to recite the names of the Twelve Minor Prophets. They are minor because they wrote short books, in contrast to Isaiah, Jeremiah and Ezekiel, who wrote long ones. I started to recite the names. Fifty years ago I learned a sort of sing-song, adding a rhythm if not much tune to the recitation. The books, the names of the books, came in sets of four. I remembered the last four first—"Zephaniah, Haggai, Zechariah, Malachi." I dragged up the first four—"Hosea, Joel, Amos, Obadiah." The middle four had me stumped—this was in the dream—I recalled, "Jonah, Nahum, Habakkuk," but there was another one, the first one in this series. I was stumped.

I woke up, thinking about it, trying to remember—not Daniel. Daniel isn't one of The Twelve—he wrote his in Aramaic, or someone did, later— It's funny what a body *can* remember. I looked it up in the morning when I got up. I'd forgotten Micah— "Micah, Jonah, Nahum, Habakkuk." How could I forget Micah? No! It's "Jonah, Micah…"

I decided to read all Twelve. And here I am in Hosea, who tells how he married a harlot, and named his children after his sermon topics. "Not-pitied," for example. Named a kid, "Not-pitied," he did, because God is not going to pity the idolatrous northern kingdom of Israel—they're doomed to be wiped out by the Assyrians. Can you imagine the mother calling the kid to come home from playing in the plaza outside? "Suppertime, Not-pitied! Come for supper!"

He named another one, "Not-my-people"—because God no longer regarded that doomed northern kingdom as his people. That's sucking the kids into the father's calling a little overmuch, I'd say. "Hey, Not-my-people! Bedtime! Come take your bath!"

I'm glad I didn't do *that* to my kids. It was bad enough as it was. The oldest, Mary, is involved in church as an adult and mother, but doesn't seem really worried that I am not. The two younger boys are not involved, and not at all interested in the institution. One of the two has indicated a wish that he knew the Biblical lore more than he does, but hasn't done anything about it that I know of. None of the three seem to be too badly scarred by the fact that they lived their earliest years in that spotlight as preacher's kids. I think I quit in time.

I remember an incident from when I was quitting. We were moving out of the manse into a house my wife had bought, and a cousin came visiting. *Her* husband was a pastor in the Evangelical United Brethren Church. She was alarmed that I seemed to have lost my faith in God. She asked Mark, the youngest, age eight, "Do you believe in God?"

His answer was totally uncoached by me, at least consciously or deliberately. "Which God?" To this day I believe it is the wisest answer possible.

Mark was involved in an earlier incident that added fuel to the fire that was cooking my spirit, preparing me for the decision to quit. A parishioner asked him, when he was about five maybe, "What do you want to be when you grow up?"

"A preacher," he said. "So I can scream at people." Everybody laughed but me. It made me very thoughtful. I mean, where'd he get that idea?

So I'm rereading the prophets and feeling kin to them. Sometimes I, like them, feel totally alienated from the culture that I am in. I am sick of the military solution to all problems, "Let's go bomb somebody…" The confusion as to whom to bomb, or whether it even matters much, except to the people who are being shelled and sniped, verges on the comical. Kill 'em. Blow 'em up. Set fire to 'em. Prove that we're better, including morally better. Evidently if they're killed by crap dropped from an American airplane, it's no moral offense.

As the last few sentences indicate, I am sick of it, divorced from it, out of it. The military is the most offensive to me, but what the military is designed to "defend," when it's anything at all except their own budget, alienates me further. They defend Americans' God-given right to steal other people's oil, trees, coffee, bananas, labor and lives. Destroy the world, so that "the American way of life," which amounts to consuming the world itself, can continue at an ever increasing rate. They call it "growth."

Not-my-people. I'll say. They're not my people. How can I separate myself from them? There's no way. When I try retreating to cultivate my own little garden, as Voltaire's Candide suggested long ago, there's this message, this indignation, this fire burning in my bones, and I am weary with keeping it in, and I cannot.

So it infects my writing. My plays and novels are didactic, like George Bernard Shaw's. When I'm told to remove that spirit from them, I am totally perplexed—that's what art is for, isn't it? If you need entertaining *only*, suck your thumb. My short stories are labeled, "delightful, but not for publication, because they are parables." Ah, yes, indeed they are. They're what the Muse brings to me. Here I stand, I can do no other.

So I write, as Hosea and Amos and Micah—don't dare forget Micah!—and especially Jeremiah wrote, not for "publication," but to record a Message. Why me? I feel like Moses in the desert when he was being called. "Oh, Lord, send some other person!" But it does no good to suggest that. This spirit, this fire, whatever it is, it is inexorable and irresistible.

21. TEACHER

In 1966 I left the church and spent the next ten years teaching in private schools, grades five through twelve, in Albuquerque. I had not been a good pastor—there was too much of the social-critic/prophet in me, not enough inclination to comfort, not enough capacity to chant, "Peace, peace," when there was no peace.

I believe I was a good teacher, even though I never took a university-sponsored education course in my life. During the last years in the church I had attended three annual Young Pastors Conferences, and I credit them with helping prepare me to become a good teacher. At the first conference I recall being exposed to a stunning new concept—that of "openness." Somehow it carried over into my teaching career, better than it ever had into my role as clergy/prophet.

Teaching felt like my true "ministry," more useful to humanity than all the clerical posturing had ever been. I was turned loose with sixth-grade boys that first year, sixteen of them at a time. I learned from them. I listened to them. I was open to them. Whenever I trotted over to the office of the Director of Studies with some sort of problem, he answered me, "Harry, play it by ear." Over and over, he told me the same thing. "You'll just have to play it by ear, Harry." So I learned to do exactly that. I listened, and did what seemed both natural and necessary, according to what I heard.

I was supposed to teach my English classes how to write. I assigned them the task of writing me a letter, once a week, in a spiral notebook. I took them home over the weekend and answered every letter, writing into each boy's notebook.

"You can laugh, Sir. You're different," they told me. Different? Other teachers can't, or don't, laugh? I began to spot something familiar, something I called "the office" back in church days. In the minds of the boys, some of them, and some of the faculty, too, there was a specialness about the teacher that had an odor similar to that of the clergy. The teacher was different from other normal human beings. Or, let's try to persuade the innocent little things to think so. I had no interest in that, and did not take part, just as I hadn't when I was a clergyman.

At pre-semester faculty meetings in the fall, the word was, "Be tough. Especially on the first day. Be stern and unquestionably in charge. You can always lighten up later." I never agreed with that advice and didn't follow it.

The special office of teacher kept coming up. We were studying *Gulliver's Travels*, the original, not the bowdlerized Sunday School version. I didn't select it—it was on the required list that was handed to me as school began. We plowed into it. The kids loved the scatological sections, where on one occasion, Gulliver, feeling great embarrassment, defecates under a cabbage leaf in Brobdignag. Another time, he offends the Queen of Lilliput, even as he saves her very life, by urinating on the palace fire. We discussed it. "Yes, the Governor pees in a pot. So does the President. The Pope craps daily, or needs to." One wide-eyed boy was experiencing a revelation. "Really, Sir? Really! It's a little hard to imagine. Even you."

"Even me, what?"

"Well, Sir, I can't imagine you having to go to the bathroom!"

Embarrassed titters sounded in the room. I declared, "Believe me, George, I do. I do." And then we all laughed. I was glad it had already been noted that I could laugh.

I learned from the boys. They brought me books, and I read them, and learned important things. Many of them learned to read, or rather learned to like to read, by being in the class. I read to them. I read in front of them, while they were doing their work at their desks. I encouraged them, and gave them credit, for reading anything. "*Opening Chess Moves*—can I read that?"

"Certainly, John. Does it interest you?"

"Yeah!"

They helped me find the myths of the world. Together we discovered poetry. Somehow I had missed it, the magic in it, when I was getting my Phi Beta Kappa memorial 95s in English Literature at Lafayette College. The boys loved for me to read *Story Poems* aloud, while they followed in their own copies of the same book. "Casey at the Bat." "Lord Randall." "The Listeners." "The Cremation of Sam Magee."

One day I asked them to get out a clean sheet of paper, in preparation for something. "Does this count, Sir?" one asked. It was a high pressure school and even sixth-graders were worried, unduly I thought, about the academic record needed to get into Harvard.

I glared at the student, and then around the room, and then back. "Every breath you take counts, Kid," I growled. But they knew I was kidding. And they knew it was somehow true, also.

I learned from the kids. One boy, son of a dentist, used to tell me as I lit up my pipe near the end of the class period, when they were going to start their homework and I was going to read up front in silence, "That's not good for you, Sir."

"I know, Brian."

Every day, the same signal. "You shouldn't do that, Sir. It'll hurt you."

"I know, Brian."

One day he brought in from his father's office brochures in living color showing step-by-step the surgical procedure for the removal of cancer of the lip and cancer of the tongue. I looked at them and took the pipe from my mouth. "OK, Brian, you win!" I exclaimed, and threw the pipe into the wastebasket, causing a loud metallic clang, which startled all the class. They watched a grown man quit smoking, for life.

After I had been there for several years, the history department allowed me to draw on my area of former expertise—the Bible. I taught a one-semester course on the Old Testament, to ninth-graders. I called it, "The History and Literature of Ancient Israel." They called it, "Sex and Violence with Good Old Mr. Willson." It did us all good, I believe. I reprocessed much of it for myself, reconfirming the humanness of the book. And I taught the boys a new way of reading—textual analysis. Keep your eye on the author. Watch out for the editor, the one the seminary professors called "the redactor." Whenever a boy asked me, "Why did God do such-and-such?" I interrupted him.

"Wait, wait, Robert. Wrong question. No one can answer that question. No one can get at that question at all. The correct question is, 'Why does the text say what it says?' And that question is important in all your reading, not just the Bible."

I taught the younger boys how to read the newspaper, borrowing an idea from Daniel Boorstin, of all people. He distinguished between events and what he called pseudo-events. This was back in the '60s. What would he say now, with "Public Relations" and "lobbying" and "dirty tricks" and plain old "lying" determining so much of policy and practice in government and media?

An event is something that happened—a hurricane, a volcanic eruption, a flood, a shooting, a drought, a plane wreck. A pseudo-event is what someone said—a meeting, an announcement, an announcement of a future meeting at which someone will say something. Press releases are pseudo-events. News conferences are pseudo-events.

The boys brought newspapers; we pasted the front page of each one on the wall, over a period of some weeks, with the stories that were pseudo-events blacked out. Day after day. It astonished all of us. Very few events were being reported. Perhaps very few events were occurring. We began to understand that "news" is not what it pretends to be. The smarter ones began to practice textual criticism on the newspaper, to watch out for the author and the editor. Who is saying all this? Who wants us to think what? It was fun.

One afternoon I suddenly found myself in a sort of reenactment of Elijah's test on Mount Carmel. The Vietnam War was raging. Our government was shooting students here in the USA. Pious frauds in high places were berating "hippies" and "peaceniks." I cannot recall the exact chain of comments in the class that led up to it, but suddenly I was raving.

"I reject the all-white, red-blooded American war god! I defy him! I *spit on him!*" One of our spring thundershowers was cruising up the mesa toward the mountains behind the school. As I yelled, "I spit on him!" a loud thunderclap boomed, startling me and frightening some of the boys. Others were jiggling in their seats in delight. Silence. "I spit on him," I repeated very quietly.

"Sir—" one boy started, then stopped. Silence.

There was no Voice. No one heeded, no one answered.

The school gave me a chance to teach "mythology" to seniors. I intended to use dreams, our dreams, which we would record and share with each other, and insights from the old Marathon experience. I did not want us to be hindered by grades. I announced, "If I give you all A's, the office will catch on, and raise Cain. So, if any of you need an A, to get into Harvard, or to preserve your all-A record, come to me at the end of class, and say so, and I'll give you the A you need. The rest will get B's, and that will be the last time we discuss grades for this entire semester." Two needed A's, and the rest were content, and we all learned a great deal, about ourselves and the world.

My way of teaching and relating to the students made the administration uneasy. Students confided things to me that would have startled parents and school officials. I refused to tell things that I knew, even when asked. I enjoyed the boys, but never knew from one year to the next whether I'd be allowed back to continue. At the end of the seventh year at the Boys' Academy, I asked for permission to break my contract and move over to the Girls' School. It was granted, and that summer both schools went co-ed.

In my new position, they wanted me to do exactly what I did and liked to do with kids. They wanted me to do a great deal of it, and in three years they worked me to death. It was another burnout. I was out of gas. I couldn't continue.

I began to wonder, again, if I wasn't trying to do what can't be done and doesn't need to be done. Any one teacher knows only a small percentage of what there is to know. Take a number—let's say I as teacher know one percent of the sum total of human knowledge. The number is too large, I know, but let's use it in order to continue supposing. Why should I, as teacher, spend so much effort pounding my one percent into these kids' heads? Who says my one percent is that all-fired important? Too much energy is spent by teachers trying to make clones of themselves out of the kids placed in their charge. The most I can do, as teacher, is point the way, open doors, suggest where to look, motivate to want to look.

For myself, I created a parable, a take-off on a scene in *Pilgrim's Progress*. Helper is standing by the Path, or coming down the Path toward Pilgrim. "May I help you?" He takes some of Pilgrim's bundles and carries them a little way. Then he hands them back, and shows Pilgrim the Path up the mountain.

"You're not going?" Pilgrim asks.

"Oh, no. I'm here to help. I may come later."

Pilgrim climbs a while, then rests and looks back. He watches Helper as he greets people, helping them in his fussy superficial way. He notices that Helper is not going up the Path. He is actually going *down* it, toward new victims he can help.

I felt a strong inner urge to be on my own pilgrim journey.

There were things I had to do, inside myself. I needed to go on up the Path. There were things "inside there" that needed to be tended to. So, being out of gas anyway, I quit. "To write." Many thought I had simply gone insane.

To write what? I wasn't sure. I started on my dreams and memories. But, why? I asked myself that, and still do. Why write? There are enough books already, too many. What needs writing? What do I know that anyone else in the world needs to know? Once again, what makes my one percent so special?

I was obsessed. I built up a body of work. Children's stories, poems, essays, short stories, novels, plays. Much of it has a sociopolitical sting in it. Much of it has a sort of philosophical angle, dealing with what I call "the big questions." Some of it, I notice now, later, stands as a kind of witness that not everyone in these times approved of the goings on, not everyone preferred Death—for forests and whales and humanity—to Life. Not everyone believed the lies. Not everyone bought into the dream of nonstop consumption of the very planet itself in the name of profit. The record is there, for what it's worth.

This teacher has a small problem. He has no one to teach. The Buddha had that problem, too. He commented that the insight he had gained was very hard to share. I don't think the Buddha wrote any books. Jesus, for sure, didn't. But the old prophets did, and I still think of myself as somehow one of them.

So, the writing has been described as "didactic," still trying to teach something, not satisfied just to entertain. I have often said, "If I'm going to ask for the privilege of taking that much of a person's attention, to read a novel, let's say, I feel obligated to provide something for that person to think about afterward."

What, for instance? What does this stuff teach? Openness. Candor. Wonder. Love of the earth, the biosphere. Magic. "Something there is, that doesn't love a wall," or nerve gas, or malnutrition, or playing with radiation. A warning. A witness.

Signposts along the path, where I've already been, maybe. Why fiction? Why so much fiction? There is magic in stories, in storytelling. Information no longer convinces. That secret place inside people can be reached by stories, by myth, not by piling up information.

Sometimes I feel like I'm the only one doing this, although I know I'm not. I find others, or signs of their passing ahead of me, every once in a while.

George Bernard Shaw has been an inspiration to me. His introductions are as exciting for me as his plays. Yet he insisted on fiction, on stories, on what he called "art." People asked him, as they asked Jesus and John Bunyan, why they taught the people in parables, through stories, through art. And he replied, like his mentors, "Art is the only way the people can be taught."

Shaw's sense of justice shines through in all his plays. He never tried to leave it out or take it out of his work. He scoffed at those who objected to "didactic" art. He scorned artists who didn't believe in anything, but simply held up a mirror to humanity, including Shakespeare and Dickens. Talk about *"el que tiene credo."* He had it, and it showed in his art.

Unabashedly, I would be like him. My plays and novels and short stories come from a point of view, and even "make a point," which labels them "didactic."

I have been frustrated by critics who label my plays "religious." One even had to mention, instead of reviewing the play, that the playwright "spent several years as a minister." It seemed to be intended to prevent thought or discussion about the basic notion, in that particular play, that "God is a metaphor, but The Whole Thing is all right." Most plays don't deal with that topic. And even though everything in the play was *anti*-religious, the play was labeled "religious," because of the theme, because it mentioned "God" and belief in "God."

Another play, a remythologization of the story of Jonah,

modernized and anachronistic at the same time, was refused by more than one theater, with the comment, "We don't do religious plays." But the play is *anti*-religious. One of the key lines is, "Gods are a pain in the ass," and the speaker, who is the real prophet in the story, includes that mean and narrow-minded God of Jonah's. Jonah isn't the prophet—the prophet is the author of the Book of Jonah. But because the play is based on four little chapters from the Bible, it is passed over as "religious."

So, this message thing that hangs on, that will not let me go, begins to feel like a hindrance, and makes me feel more than ever kin to old Jeremiah. He called his problem "God," and I do not, which adds to the complication and confusion. *He* said, "If I say, 'I will not mention him, or speak any more in his name,' there is in my heart as it were a burning fire shut up in my bones, and I am weary with holding it in, and I cannot." I know that feeling. It comes over me every time I pick up a pen—not "God," but—what? Truth. Justice. Love. I'm not the only one loyal to those things. So why does it feel so lonely?

22. LANGUAGE

In this day of finer and finer specialization, I think of myself as a generalist. All too often I see evidence that the scoffer's definition of an expert is basically true: "One who knows more and more about less and less, culminating in one who knows all there is to know about nothing." I love to see connections, to jump disciplines, to mix or confuse genres. The obvious danger is the other scoffer's definition: "Jack of all trades and master of none."

If one could do life over, there's no doubt I would be strongly tempted to specialize in my most obvious aptitude—language. I still recall the thrill of holding that Latin textbook in my hand on the first day in the ninth grade. It was magic. I had a similar sensation when I first opened *Finnegan's Wake*—it looks like English, but it isn't, it's another language.

My mother came to this country from Scotland when she was sixteen. Her accent was thick, and her vocabulary enriched mine. To this day Scottish words come to mind, in word games, and my chicana wife is chagrined that they indeed appear in the English dictionary. "They belong in a Scottish dictionary!"

My father had been certified as a teacher of high school German, and he claimed that, because of his efforts, I was virtually bilingual the summer I was three. I do not remember that, but do remember the sensation that came to me often when I studied German in college. It was all vaguely familiar, and it felt like I was re-learning something.

In seminary, "the original languages" were the bugaboo of many, perhaps most, of my classmates. They struggled through minimum requirements and hated it. I gobbled it up, first Greek, then Hebrew. Most of my elective courses were Biblical studies in the original languages.

Then came the opportunity to go to Spain, which I assumed would be language preparation for a lifetime abroad as a missionary. I had had two years of poorly taught Spanish in high school, and with the German, Greek and Hebrew piled on in the meantime, I had forgotten all of it. When we got off the plane in Madrid, I did not know how to ask for a glass of water. Our whole family underwent immersion.

My task was to learn the language, I thought, so I did. I had two tutors a day. I read only Spanish. I prepared vocabulary notebooks. I learned to listen.

I made what some regarded to be remarkable progress. One of the tutors assigned a task in writing every day. The other took us out into the city—on the metro, to the market, to the Gran Via, to the zoo, to the Prado Museum. He pointed, he spoke, enunciating clearly. He corrected, but did not bother with grammatical explanations. The other tutor did that. We went to the movies. We saw the same movie over and over, until the plot was clear, and every time we sat through it we picked up more vocabulary.

The verb began to come, as second nature, without having to think first, "preterite, first person plural indicative." I found myself talking to myself as I rode the subway, or walked the streets, in Spanish. I was ready with questions when the tutor appeared: "*¿Cómo se dice—?*"

The subjunctive was elusive, but a light went on as I listened to my three-year-old daughter, who became bilingual with no effort very early on. We were going out for the evening, leaving her with a babysitter. *"No quiero que tú vayas,"* she told her mother, ("I do not want that you should go"). On another occasion she warned a visiting child, who was hammering on a peg board, while her newborn baby brother lay in a low-slung buggy nearby, *"Cuidado, que no hagas daño a Andy."* ("Careful, that you not do harm to Andy.") That's how you learn, Harry, by listening.

I learned to listen to people in a new way. Not, "Why do they say that?" No, not trying to see the logic, or impose my logic on their language. Rather, simply, "How do they say it?"

I found cultural arrogance, in myself, and in most fellow Americans. I tended to dislike and avoid the latter group in Spain. "How much is this in real money?" I heard them ask, shouting as if the clerk was deaf. I've seen them laugh in restaurants, riffling through the pile of peseta notes they were leaving as a tip, indicating their low opinion of the value. I began to reevaluate what I had been taking completely for granted—the so-called American way of life, which was becoming a slogan about then. It was *a* way of doing things, but not *the* way, maybe not the best way, certainly not the only way.

My discoveries deepened. There are things you can say in one language that you cannot say in any other way. You have to know the language in order to say them. *"No me da la gana."* "I don't feel like it,"—but that's not exactly it. *"Tengo ganas..."* "I feel like..."—but, no, not quite, you're missing something. *"¡Viva yo!"* "Long live me!"—clumsy, ungrammatical, you can't say it in English.

I came to believe that really learning the second language performed a kind of surgery in the brain, doubling the number of nerve endings. I know in my case, it did me much, much good. It had to do with "openness," even though I only came across that word for it some years later. Closed persons, closed-minded, uptight persons—these do not do well in learning new languages.

A strange thing happened to me as I was outgrowing all my Christian theologies and about to leave the church. I found myself distinguishing between English Harry and Spanish Harry. I was a little startled to find that Spanish Harry was more conservative, and slower to change, than English Harry. I suppose the explanation lay in the language I was reading mostly and the function played by my ability to preach and pray aloud in Spanish.

The Spanish language in the Presbyterian churches of New Mexico had become an enclave of the past, a bastion of ways that were dying, or had already died. *"Esto es México,"* one of the stubborn old elders told me. One of the great ironies of my life is that I, who love the Spanish language so much and am so grateful for what learning it did for me, became the agent of its removal from the Presbyterian churches in New Mexico. I had learned Spanish from members of La Iglesia Evangélica, a group who were living in a New Testament situation, complete with Caesar and catacombs. They were mostly Neo-orthodox, if one must label them, and some were not nearly that "liberal." I respected and loved them, but they were seven thousand miles away when I was in my crisis, and my theological feet were on slippery ground. So, Spanish Harry was more conservative, as English Harry whipped through the history of Christian theology and right on out the door.

My study of Spanish enhanced my love and appreciation of

English. When I resumed reading English, about half-way through that year in Spain, I was reading more than twice as fast, and voraciously demanding "input." My practical tutor, a student at the seminary only a little older than I, was learning English. "You like English," I noted. "Why?"

"*Porque con pocas palabras se dice mucho.*" "Because with few words one can say a lot." I agreed. English does require fewer syllables than Spanish to say the same thing. We had noted it already in the Lord's Prayer and the 23rd Psalm. I gained a new appreciation for English, especially the Anglo-Saxon roots and all those monosyllables. Rudolph Flesch told all about it in *The Art of Plain Talk*. I preached that way. Later I taught that way. I still write that way. Clarity, clarity, clarity. "If I speak with the tongues of men and of angels and have not *clarity...*" Dr. Hope used to insist on that in seminary; he was the same professor who taught us that all Presbyterian ministers were equal, but that some were more equal than others.

I studied the so-called four-letter words in English and wondered why they were so much more potent than their Latinate counterparts. "Flatulent, urinate, defecate, copulate"—no big deal, no reaction. But the Anglo-Saxon equivalents are Magic Words. I have concluded that the magic was caused by the Norman defeat of the Anglo-Saxons in 1066. This is all laid out in the Magic Word Pages of a play/novella of mine called *This'll Kill Ya: The Last Word on Censorship*. The verbs are conjugated, to the delight of some of the audience and the consternation of censors, who turn up in every crowd.

Spanish has a kind of delightful vulgarity. The language accepts the fact that we are in bodies. It takes a little getting used to, but I thoroughly enjoyed it. Spanish also takes horrible sideswipes at irrational authority, stuffed shirts and sacred cows. *"Viva yo"* contributes to that.

I came to New Mexico with the conviction that I had not learned

Spanish for nothing. Then, while here, I used less and less Spanish, and finally none. I still have to wonder about that sometimes. Why *did* I learn it? I'm convinced it changed me, opened me, made me susceptible to the growth that was to follow. But as a salable skill, it has never borne fruit. Perhaps it's better that way.

Our home is bilingual. Adela uses more Spanish than I, but I understand her, and continue to learn new nuances. I think she would not have become my wife had I not known Spanish. I choose my words carefully.

"How can you say I'm not a gringo?"

"You're not."

"What's a gringo? What makes me *not* one?"

"You know the language."

Aha! So, I have not learned Spanish for nothing, and if that's all I have to show for it, she's the Pearl of Great Price.

I wish everyone could have the doubled-nerve-ending operation. The Treaty of Guadalupe Hidalgo says that New Mexico is supposed to be bilingual, but it isn't. I imagine truly bilingual schools, in which students and teachers really do not know or care or keep track of which language they are doing their work in—they'd *all* learn twice as much and twice as fast! But we don't have that. There are teachers labeled "bilingual" in special programs, for elementary school only, but they aren't. It's a sham.

I believe that language is one of the most marvelous capacities that humans have. It makes us important on some evolutionary scale, as important as dolphins. I am deeply troubled that our language is being perverted and polluted on a grand scale by government, advertising and public relations companies. Liars destroy language itself.

The Houyhnhnym in *Gulliver's Travels* is stunned when he catches Gulliver in a lie. "He said that which was not." Rational beings can hardly grasp the concept.

In the midst of my teaching years, while I was holding forth on the value of language study, I stumbled across a thesis by an anthropologist that the function of language is deceit. Body language doesn't lie, but words lie. That's what they're *for*, he proposed. Bees and rivers and mountains and trees and galaxies don't lie. But humans, with their gift of language, use it to excuse, to brag, to cheat, to deceive, to deny, to say that which is not. Is that what the language is for? Surely, not.

23. SCIENCE AND NATURE

Preparation for medical school required taking science classes, because in those days a doctor was a scientist. I became a chemistry major at Lafayette College, with minors in mathematics and biology. The clarity and precision thrilled me—questions did have answers. I was good at memorizing things like the periodic table of the elements, formulae and equations, phylum/class/order lists, the names of bones and nerves. I was good at following my nose down the trail of inferences in analytic geometry and calculus. And Dr. Kunkle's challenge to follow Truth wherever it led became deeply imbedded in me.

I did well in science courses, and allowed the insistence on clarity and evidence to carry over into philosophical and theological studies later. My training in science was useful in seminary. I relished textual analysis and "word studies," and was suspicious of foggy thinking and irrational authority. Truth never was linked to ecclesiastical authority for me, but rather had an independent existence of its own, which I thought could be ascertained by study. I did my thinking in the manner of a scientist, not a theologian. To me it was a joke from the beginning that someone once called theology the Queen of the Sciences, since the statement itself was derived from authority, not evidence.

Since I went to seminary directly after studying science in

college, and then came to New Mexico as a missionary-pastor right after finishing seminary, I never held a job as a paid practicing scientist. But I never gave up the habits of thinking that the study of science gave me. In fact, I have found myself using them in my long-term observations of science itself.

New Mexico has been home to many scientists since the 1950s. We have a remarkable proportion of Ph.D.s in nuclear physics, M.D.s, Ph.D.s in computer science. Much of the activity of these scientists is called "research." They are widening the circle of human knowledge, pushing back that great barrier called "The Unknown." Over decades the vast majority of these scientists have been paid by the Pentagon to do weapons research, and they have done their work in secret. Ordinary citizens "off-base" or "off-lab" have no clear knowledge of what these scientists are, and have been, doing.

The anecdotal material that does come to us does not reassure us much. An acquaintance of ours was honored for inventing special fuses for bombs, which prevented their exploding in the jungle canopy of Vietnam, where they killed monkeys only. The new fuses insured that the bombs exploded on the ground where people were. Other friends work on miniaturization of atomic bomb detonators and other parts so that they can be carried in a briefcase. Others invent laser ray guns, which melt holes in ten-inch steel. Many do computer simulations of bomb and shell trajectories. Lab employees told us of spy-satellite photography that could reveal the writing on the newspaper that Nikita Kruschev was reading.

"What do you do all day?" I asked a friend, who seemed to be a sensitive person in other areas. He has a Ph.D. in mathematics.

"They put a problem in front of us. We solve it."

"You don't think about how it fits into the larger picture?"

"We don't see the larger picture. I only think about that here at the supper table with a margarita. Over there, it's just a problem, and the thrill of solving it."

It reminded me of an anecdote told about J. Robert Oppenheimer, head of the Manhattan Project in Los Alamos. As a boy he was not a good baseball player because he was distracted by his need to calculate in his head the velocity of the ball, instead of hitting it, or running. Science can be detached from real life all too easily, and it seems to have been purchased by war interests, especially here in New Mexico.

The medical establishment in New Mexico is huge and highly regarded. It began as tuberculosis sanitoria and research, long before the Manhattan Project and all the subsequent weapons research. Now cancer research is big business here. It concerns some of us that the search seems to be centered on trying to cure it after people have it, rather than on preventing it or identifying and removing the causes of it. Some of us clear-thinking cynics suspect a linkage between the radiation-and-weapons business and the lack of interest in cancer prevention.

Not all scientists have been purchased, but those who have make for dramatic news. The tobacco companies have found and hired "scientists" who state flatly that there is no proven connection between smoking and any health problem. *All* subjects, so far, die anyway, eventually, so the statistics that suggest linkage can still be questioned.

The Department of Energy has found and hired "scientists" who state categorically that the underground salt depository, designed for the transuranic waste produced in the manufacture of nuclear weapons over the past fifty years, will not leak radiation into the environment for ten thousand years. Promises like that sound very unscientific to us amateurs. What about earthquakes? There has been one already, while we protestors tried to hinder the planned opening of the facility. What about brine? Water seeps out of the salt beds, in spite of assertions that there was no water there. What kind of steel drums will resist corrosion for ten thousand years? And, besides, the half-life of that material indicates that it will be

Prophet With No God 117

lethal for 250,000 years. What kind of scientist would think that burying it was a good idea? Perhaps amateur scientists and nonscientists are not supposed to understand the concept of half-life. A purchased scientist can be paid to say anything. His "science" does not protect him, or us, from corruption. Science, as such, is becoming suspect. In my youth I had to go through the great debate that science was anti-God and anti-Bible. For me, science won, really, because I identified science with Truth. But now we have a new debate. "Science" has become anti-human. I need the quotation marks because I'm referring to corrupted science, purchased science.

In the third voyage of Lemuel Gulliver—*The Voyage To La Puta*, Jonathan Swift made fun of the fact that scientists are and have long been purchasable. Pronounce the title correctly, with a Spanish accent, and very few New Mexicans will misunderstand. Even gringos know that "*puta*" means "whore." Kings and academies have purchased the experimenters that Swift mocks so mercilessly. Science is a whore, he says. She does for money what she should do for love—search out facts, ascertain Truth, add to our understanding of the world we are in.

The image of the modern scientist, as used by print and television advertisers, has become the new irrational authority. The scientist has replaced the medieval priest. Depict someone in a white lab coat recommending something—a laxative, a tire, a cold "remedy"—and it will sell. People will believe and obey what scientists tell them. And the fact that we cynics know that these persons in white coats aren't scientists at all but merely actors, paid actors who will say what they are paid to say, only adds to our frustration.

But a worm is turning. The reputation of science is tarnished. The cartoon image of the mad scientist has been around for more than a century. The nuclear bomb business has left our nation so badly polluted, you'd think there had been a nuclear war here. We aren't sure the same group can be trusted to clean it up, since the scientists and their employers have lied so much about it already.

And now the news of Buchenwald-on-the-Rio-Grande begins to break. American citizens were injected with plutonium, in experiments that smell like Auschwitz, without their knowledge, with a view to learning things about radioactivity and the human body. A fellow scientist of the doctor who did some of the injections defended the practice by saying of him, "He is not a monster. He is not a ghoul. He is a scientist." But not everyone thinks that settles the matter. It sounds like a clue.

Science has become the new irrational authority. Science has been regarded as infallible. Science has been allowed to transcend human life, human lives, human morality and Truth itself. But not everyone is pleased, not anymore.

Many thoughtful people have noted that modern technology, which is made possible by science, has outrun humanity's moral development. Gulliver tells how the Houyhnhnm figured it out clearly enough. "He said, 'he had been very seriously considering my whole story, as far as it related both to myself and my country; that he looked upon us as a sort of animal to whose share, by what accident he could not conjecture, some small pittance of reason had fallen, whereof we made no other use, than by its assistance, to aggravate our natural corruptions, and to acquire new ones, which nature had not given us…'"

The plutonium injections seem amateurish from this latter-day perspective. What did they hope to learn? Did they learn it? The explainers refer to "resulting radiation standards," but we know that these can be and are changed as the universal dosage increases because of "classified" activities, and that there is nothing scientific about "standards."

Other fields of research and experimentation are outpacing humanity's "moral development," or even legal considerations, which are far from being the same thing. Legality has been used so

Prophet With No God

far to protect business and government, not to define or defend any moral value. Organ transplants and the need for organs will yet lead to abuses that will remind us of Dachau. The Senator needs a liver. This shoplifter doesn't need his. And here's this Sandinista...

Gene implantation is already leaking out of the laboratory and into the cows and the milk we drink. We used to think that the scientists would save us from all our problems, if only they'd hurry with their research. The clamor for AIDS research echoes that old idea. Now some of us are not so confident of science. Some of us are downright suspicious. I personally will not be in any way surprised to learn that the AIDS virus is man-made, paid for by one secret budget or another. Biological warfare is *still* in the budget.

We are alarmed at what science has enabled technology to do to nature. Commercial ocean fishing, for example, with radar and miles-long drift nets, is rapidly emptying the ocean of life itself. Forestry, with machines that remove *everything*, is converting much of the earth into a desert. The whales are doomed. So are the rivers. So are we, perhaps. Our science has outstripped not only our moral development, it has outstripped any sense of self-preservation as a species or a biosphere.

We must be thankful that there are still some unpurchased scientists left—they're the ones alarmed about the ozone layer, massive species extermination, global warming and oxygen depletion caused by human activity. Notice how the polluters hire other "scientists" to mock these pioneers and pooh-pooh their findings. The unpurchased scientists are called "alarmists" and "special interests" by the mockers, but some of us find the information frankly alarming, and perhaps understated. Additional alarm is badly needed.

It is no accident that "Modern Western Science," as it is called, developed in the culture that had been permeated with Christianity. The Christian attitude toward "nature" was excellent preparation for the heartless probing that was necessary and the "conquest" that has followed. Animists believe that nature is alive; scientists cease noting that the animals and plants and humans that they are experimenting on are alive. Christians condemned and still condemn nature-worship as idolatry. Yet the forests were safer from utter annihilation when the humans worshipped them. Now that forests are no more than so many board-feet of profit-making lumber, they and their inhabitants are at great risk.

I learned to love the creeks and trees and hills when I was a boy. I forgot them for a while, when I worked my way through Christianity. Now I am back, and find my attitude toward the biosphere more animistic than I would have ever suspected. It is not hard for me to imagine the cry of anguish of an ancient tree as it and all its companions are slaughtered. I lament, personally, the destruction of the whales and dolphins. I feel the Native American sense of sacrilege when an ecosystem is destroyed by roads and bridges and chain saws and plows.

Christianity was a bad myth, with its notion of human domination over the earth and its creatures. Christianity and science—that is, science as it has come to be in our time—go hand in hand in bringing about the destruction of the planet we are living on. To call those of us who care about all this "environmentalists" and then dismiss us as a "special interest group" is a clever trick that flies in the face of logic. The profit-taking destroyers are the special interest group, and not large in number. With the environment destroyed, nothing else survives. The only thing "special" about that interest is that there are so few willing to raise any fuss about it.

Sometimes it is tempting for me to assume that I must not only get over Christianity, but also science. And yet, as a method of thought, and an insistence on clarity and evidence, I regard my use of science as a good and helpful thing. Part of my study of myth, by which I finally got over Christianity, included what was called "scientific introspection."

I examined some material that most modern scientists dismiss with a laugh: Tarot cards, runes, totems, astrology. All of it was a kind of science in its heyday, and it still is, with this important difference—the subject of study is oneself, one's inner life. All of that material, all the meaning of all those symbols, is within each one of us, and the one subject that I could thoroughly study was myself. The one instance of human nature that I could examine was myself. The one example of human intelligence that I could keep track of was myself.

In order to do this study, I had to fend off old voices that said, "My, you're sure preoccupied with yourself!" Indeed, I was. I had discovered that the one human life I was fully responsible for, and the only one I could change at all, was myself. I needed to understand my subject. Scientific introspection, it was. The study, the work, is not completed. This enquiry is a small part of it. There is no recognized branch of science called introspection. I'll never become Chairman of the Department of Scientific Introspection at some university. But science is still alive and well, unpurchased, in this exercise that will keep me busy for the rest of my life.

The other brand of science that nourishes my sense of wonder is astronomy. This one is recognized, although profit-takers are admittedly puzzled about what it is *for*. The "space program," which does have a remarkable budget, is not astronomy. I only do astronomy second hand, but I regard it as important, and derive much personal good from it. The size of the cosmos, the time, the distances, the puzzles hinted at way out there, black holes, great walls—and the minds struggling to grasp and comprehend, with no way of converting the findings to personal profit—there's something in all that that I honor.

In my backyard I have a parable of this wonder—a beehive. The bees are remarkable. The collective intelligence is mysterious. Could such a thing happen to us? Are we evolving in that direction? Not if you judge by the leaders we've been picking lately. The bees are patently marvelous, but, then, so also is the fact that humans are figuring out what the bees are doing. I do that, and then feel humbled by my own awareness of the process. And it's a kind of science. I do take honey, as my share of the profit.

24. SOCIAL PROTEST

On the 25th anniversary of the murder of Martin Luther King, which was also the 50th anniversary of the establishment of Los Alamos National Laboratory, I took part in a civil action. My companions were Quakers, peace activists, environmentalists, persons with a high sense of social responsibility. The Department of Energy, which replaced the Atomic Energy Commission and runs the lab, has a security regulation that forbids leafleting at the facility. We decided in the name of the right of sovereign citizens to engage in free speech to leaflet the people who work at the lab, that is, to offer them reading material as they went in to work. We were not an organized group, salaried by internal or external enemies of the United States. We were the people of the United States, a very few of them actually, from whom all these deadly secrets are being kept. Each one of us prepared his or her own leaflet.

Mine was a short story dialogue I had written some while earlier, entitled, "Right Livelihood." The title comes from the Buddha's Eightfold Path—one of the paths is Right Livelihood. The story weaves in concerns about "jobs, jobs, jobs" with other larger questions—there *are* larger questions! Cancer, ancient forests, radioactive half-life, personal responsibility for the consequences of one's actions—compared to these things, holding a job and obeying orders in order to continue holding a job are less important, I still believe.

As I drove to Santa Fe to meet my fellow leafleters, I pondered the influence of Martin Luther King on my life. His "I Have a Dream" speech thrilled me in 1963. I took part in the march from Selma to Montgomery in 1965. I really believed in the old American ideal of equality, although since then I have come to see that most Americans do not believe in that ideal at all. My seminary thesis was based on the writings of Ernest Troeltsch and Martin Luther King.

After leaving the organized clergy, I spent the long hot summer of 1967 on the staff of the Southern Christian Leadership Conference in Atlanta. SCLC assigned me as their representative to the Atlanta Alliance for Peace, a conglomerate of all sorts of activist groups who were planning an anti-Vietnam War demonstration for Hiroshima Day.

I recalled details of that long, hot summer. There were riots in Detroit, Newark and other places. The poster on the wall in our headquarters listed the takeover of the court house in Tierra Amarilla, New Mexico by land-grant heirs as one of the "riots." The Atlanta Alliance for Peace elected me chairman, and we went to work. I put in eighteen-hour days, organizing, mobilizing, planning with the police the parade route and the rallying place.

For a time, I and everyone assumed that Martin Luther King would be the keynote speaker at the final rally, but he refused. I couldn't believe it. I pled with him and his officers—Andy Young, Hosea Williams, Ben Clarke. No. It wasn't the right time. "The war is immoral!" I yelped. "Martin knows it is."

"Sure, he does."

"The war is derailing his so-called War on Poverty, which is crucial to our goal of real equality."

"That's right."

"The war is un-American, un-Christian, illegal, unconstitutional, based on lies!" I wailed.

"Yes. We know that, but it is not the right time."

Dick Gregory was our keynote speaker, and he spoke very

clearly about the war. Hosea Williams did likewise. "They want free elections in Vietnam, and we ain't yet had free elections in Georgia!"

But Martin Luther King did not speak. He did not appear at all. We mounted the largest anti-war demonstration, to date, in Old Dixie. But I came home confused and depressed. When is the right time, if this isn't it?

The following February, King came out clearly against the war. The funneling of money and material and expertise into the destruction of the lives of colored people in Asia was undermining and preventing the enhancement of the lives of colored people here at home. I recalled the chant of the black marchers at our Hiroshima Day parade: "No Viet Cong ever called me 'nigger'!"

So, someone had decided that the right time had arrived. Two months later King was murdered. In my grief I figured out a way to blame myself a little. I had spent the previous summer adding to the pressure on him to come out against the war, and as soon as he did come out, the war people killed him.

I spent the summer of 1968 as logistics chairman of the Albuquerque Coalition for the Poor Peoples March, using much of the expertise about planning parades with police, and marshalling volunteers to do what they have committed themselves to do. I did not go to Washington, with the select few, to live in Tent City for a while. I retired from public protest activity.

Burnout. A textbook case. Drop out. Lick your wounds. "I'll lay me down and bleed for a while—then I'll rise and fight again…" It's an old Scottish ballad. But I wasn't sure I'd ever rise and fight again. I wasn't sure it did any good. All the efforts for equality did enable some blacks to become better off than before, but the majority remained in worse poverty and oppression than ever. And most whites still do not believe in equality.

All-out protest efforts demanding an end to the war did not end the war. The war people murdered Robert Kennedy, elected Nixon and Kissinger, and kept the war going with horrible slaughter, especially of Asians, for five more years. What ended the war was the protest of the veterans. I believed it then, and still believe it. "I'll never trust my government again," they said, publicly, more and more of them, throwing their Purple Hearts over the White House fence, or into bonfires, in front of TV cameras. The war ended because the Vietnamese people *won* and the Americans finally stopped killing and went home—which is exactly what some of us said had to be done, back in 1965.

It cost me my "career," but I was going to lose that anyway, so I shouldn't overstate the case now. The point now, I was thinking, as I drove to Santa Fe to take part in a tiny little right-livelihood, right-to-leaflet action, is that evidently I'm still confused about social actions.

If they don't do any good, why do I persist in doing them? I was pulled back out into the streets by plutonium, and by Eliot Abrams, whom I regard as a key incarnation of the Spirit of Evil in our time. He was the U.S. State Department under-secretary for Latin America, later pardoned by President Bush for high crimes against the people of the United States and the people of the world—he was up to his ears in Iran-Contra theft, murder and lies. Some of us knew it all the while.

The hostility of the American government under Ronald Reagan toward the people of Nicaragua and their revolution brought me back out into the streets. I took part in demonstrations and sit-ins at congressional offices. "U.S. out of Central America." "Your taxes are murdering nurses and teachers." "Ronald Reagan and Eliot Abrams are liars."

The hostility of the American government against the biosphere itself for the past fifty years, expressed in its nuclear weapons program, also brought me back from burnout and drop out. In my most cynical moments I suspect that citizen protest does no good, that the system of police-state national security and secrecy cannot be "reformed." In a strange way, it reminds me of my attitude toward reforming the church. It can't be done—we'll have to wait for it to collapse of its own fat-cat weight. We'll have to wait for the Cosmic Reversal, which may require eons of Time.

In New Mexico, the U.S. government has done much to express its hostility toward all living things. The atomic bomb was invented in Los Alamos, and they have been "improving" and "perfecting" the radioactive explosions for fifty years. They have contaminated, perhaps irretrievably, all the places where they have done that.

The first atomic bomb explosion took place in New Mexico, not Japan. Farmers and ranchers, to say nothing of the wildlife, were not warned. The test site has been used ever since for rocket missile experiments. In Albuquerque, that great city, the largest single employer is the Sandia Laboratory/Sandia Base complex, where delivery systems for the atomic weapons are invented and "perfected." The activities are all secret—the vast majority of the sovereign citizens have no idea what is really going on in there. Just east of that Base Complex, overlooking the city, the Manzano Mountains are honey-combed with underground tunnels and storage rooms where some of the 20,000-plus stockpile of nuclear weapons is kept in readiness.

The hostility of the U.S. government is all-pervasive, and not aimed at any particular enemy. The communists are sorely missed, in fact. The "enemy," the one that requires the most ingenuity and effort to deal with adequately, is the sovereign people of the United States, who must pay for all this wickedness and are already dying of the consequences of it. Cancer rates among base workers are classified! Cancer rates are secret! It is all still secret. Workers in Los Alamos get marvelous health insurance, in contrast to the rest of us, who can also breathe and ingest their loose plutonium—but it is still all secret.

And now the crowning touch. The U.S. government found an economically depressed county in New Mexico. Potash mines had been closed. There they built an underground storage facility for the nuclear waste that has resulted from the manufacture of all those nuclear weapons. They call it the Waste Isolation Pilot Project. We call it WIPP. They proposed burying in salt beds the transuranic waste from Los Alamos, Oak Ridge, Rocky Flats, Hanford, Fernal, Savannah River—all the polluted factories where the atomic bombs have been made.

A small group of citizens briefly prevented the opening of WIPP, by protest and legal action, insisting on compliance with safety regulations. I'm not a ringleader by any means, but I have been a warm body from time to time. And the question in this enquiry is: Why do you do that, Harry? You must believe in something that most of the citizens of Albuquerque and New Mexico do not. There are only a dozen of you here in Los Alamos with your leaflets. There are a couple of hundred of you altogether —and there are one and a half million residents in this state. What is it you believe, Harry, that makes you do this?

It's hard to pin down. Billy Taylor sang a song he had dedicated to Martin Luther King on the 25th anniversary of his murder. "If you really are concerned, then show it…" I try to show it. I don't do it for God, not anymore. So, then, for what?

Old words still reverberate. "Witness," for example. My novel *A World For the Meek* is a tiny, almost inaudible and invisible witness that not all of us agreed to this unrelenting hostility and poisoning. The novel will be incinerated, if these mad persons are not stopped, along with everything else. My life, my tiny little protest, is a witness that not everyone approves of this greedy insanity. But my life can be brushed aside, along with all those other beautiful fragile lives.

And what is the witness for? For whose benefit? I talk to others, who agree that the DOE budget for new atomic weapons is madness and immorality. But they don't protest. Why not?

"It doesn't do any good. They'll do what they have decided to do. They have the cops and the army and the atomic bombs on their side."

But we protestors changed the government schedule on WIPP. And they haven't hauled us away and shot us yet. We haven't, yet, joined the *desaparecidos* of Chile and Argentina and Nicaragua and El Salvador.

Something about Truth comes vaguely to mind. Something about Justice. My sister, before our final estrangement, told me she envied my certainty. She admires, a great deal, Ronald Reagan and Eliot Abrams and Jean Kirkpatrick. When she told me she envied my certainty, it brought me up short, and I thought about it. The conventional wisdom states that there are two sides to every question. I keep bumping into questions that do not have two sides!

The last whale ought *not* to be killed, no matter whose job it is to kill it or how much he's being paid to kill it or how long his family tradition has consisted of killing whales. The last redwood ought *not* to be cut down, no matter whose job is on the line. Fathers should *not* be taxed to pay for programs that give children leukemia, no matter how evil the enemy on the other side of the globe may appear to be. Material lethal to all life forms with a half-life of 25,000 years, which will still be lethal after 250,000 years, *should not be moved*, and we should not be making any more of it, for any reason whatsoever, no matter whose job is lost or how many jobs are lost on that account. And so forth...

Truth. Logic. Justice. Fairness. Whose world *is* this? Eliot Abrams'? The most efficient slaughterers'? So I drove to Santa Fe, and rode on to Los Alamos with a dozen other beautiful people, to say what it seems to me all one-and-a-half million of us ought to be saying. I must believe in something that they don't. I wonder what it is.

I keep bumping into what is called "relativism" in philosophy. There is no such thing as Truth. There are not even bad motives—everyone, *everyone*, these relativists insist, is trying to

Prophet With No God

turn a personal profit of some kind. "You want it to be black-and-white, cut-and-dried, and it never is." I hear that a great deal in response to my observation of questions that have only one side.

Maybe it's as simple as that. Most people are relativists, and I am not. When I left the church and began to study world mythology, I studied the ancient lore of the Tarot. Much of it is the old nature religion that Christianity officially replaced. Some of it is the Jewish Kabbalah, anathema to orthodox rabbis. Some of it goes back to ancient Egypt and as far away as the yogis of India. Taoism and Zen are either in it, or related to it. It is an expression of the one-world monomyth.

In studying the Tarot, I found the concept of the Undeviating Justice. It isn't a "God," who can be argued with, according to dozens of Bible stories. The Undeviating Justice is something else. Newton saw a glimpse of it. "Every action has an equal and opposite reaction." Pendulum lore has it. "The swing to the left equals the swing to the right." Holography and astrology both have it. "As above, so below." "The whole is contained in each of the parts."

No legal or justice system in the world has much to do with the Undeviating Justice, except in pretence. Bribes, loopholes, extenuating circumstances, privilege, prerogative, "insanity," motivation—no, that's not the Undeviating Justice. It's more like Nature than human law. Gravity, gravitation, the natural constants that humans are learning a little about—that's more like it. No exceptions. No excuses. No alibis.

The more the ego thinks about it, the less it likes it. But we can get beyond ego. I think that's why I instinctively call my fellow protestors "the beautiful people." They have moved a little, and some a lot, beyond ego. For myself, I wouldn't claim more than a very little. The resounding failures of life have helped in my case to provide a glimpse of that "fair country" beyond ego.

So—evidently, I believe that I, at least, need to be clear about these one-sided questions, and I'm willing to take strange unnecessary risks in order to state openly my solidarity with the one incontrovertible side on those issues— Be careful, Harry! Beware of confusion. You pretend to be beyond ego, and it looks like more ego than ever! You're slipping into Messianism. No wonder your Reaganite sister envies your certainty.

Actually, I'm not sure she really did envy my certainty. She had her own. She was simply puzzled that mine was so different from hers, so opposite. And I suffer the same puzzlement. How can she approve the blatant lying, the murder of nurses and literacy workers, the selling of weapons to avowed enemies of the country she's so loyal to?

I am stuck with my certainty and do not accept the notion that "everyone can have his own certainty," with no reality check. I still believe in my own ability to recognize truth or falsehood, cause and effect, life or death. So I must protest. I wish I had the energy to protest more.

The experience of being a missionary-pastor, active in the presbytery and in the community, has left me permanently flawed. I cannot stand gatherings of humans, what were and still are called "meetings." Committee meetings, faculty meetings, departmental meetings, in-service training meetings, neighborhood meetings, protest planning meetings—I am made ill, physically and psychologically. I have said that I could never be a Central American socialist, because I wouldn't be able to stand the endless community meetings at which consensus is being sought. Maybe I could be a dictator, but I was not good at it when I had the chance—I kept wanting the group to decide. But the group won't decide. Instead it wastes the time and energy of all its talented members in endless meetings. I have not figured out how certain things will ever get done without all the meetings, but I have figured out that I must limit my involvement. I notice that my pungent comments seem mostly unhelpful, anyway.

At times my problem seems to go deeper. I find myself disliking humans in organized groups. I find myself not approving of humans at all, whenever they act in groups. I do not believe that churches are benevolent organizations. I have become an anarchist, not believing in, or approving of, or offering any loyalty to, any government I know about, especially the one that claims authority over me.

There are many individual humans that I like, some very much. Not all the gene-pool family, I must admit. I am able to trust individuals, some of them, and I don't think I'm an unfriendly person, really, but I could never trust a church group again, or any committee, or any organized group of colleagues, or the family of siblings. I am condemned to be a loner.

For a while I thought it was a flaw I should do something about. I have never found anything helpful to do. I have tried to get involved in "the public thing" several times since partial recovery from burnout. Perhaps I choose hopeless causes, and it's as simple as that! The meeting problem drives me immediately back to the fringes. Maybe it's an irreparable flaw. Maybe it's a permanent scar. Some of it is disgust that there are so few willing to exert any effort of any kind to stop the permanent poisoning of our world. Why does that seem to matter to so few? And those precious few wasting their indignation on meetings!

I am totally put off by institutions and bureaucracy, especially large ones, like our university with more than 25,000 students, or high schools with 5,000. The telephone monopoly, the electric power and natural gas monopoly, huge for-profit hospitals, City Hall, the Motor Vehicle Licensing Department—sometimes I think my visceral disgust with all that goes back to my overdosing on meetings when I was young and full of energy.

At any rate, what I believe in does not include any faith in the ability of human vested interest groups, or contending protest groups, even in the name of love and justice and plain good sense, to solve problems.

Problems. Yes, problems. My unfaith is about to show, in full regalia. As a species, we have problems. We are an endangered species, and we are a threat to the biosphere itself. I admit to being part of the problem: I am willing to protest openly, but am unable to sit through the meetings that will be required, and I lament the fact that too few are attending to these problems. I sometimes think that if there is no Undeviating Justice, there ought to be.

25. GOD, AND ANGELS

As I found myself out on my prophetic limb, without "God," I decided that I needed to write "The History of God." A brief outline of it follows.

The natural uncomplicated religious attitude of human beings, and also the oldest and most primitive, is called "animism." The history of "God" must begin here. Animism is the belief that all the universe is alive. The rocks, the mountains, as well as the trees, the grasses, the animals, the soil, the rivers, the lakes, the ocean, the clouds, the sun, the moon, all the stars, our tools, the bricks we make our houses out of—all of it is alive and sentient. It is all "animated." A spirit lives in every thing.

Animism can develop in many directions. A nasty negative attitude can arise. The world and its contents may be regarded as hostile. The animating spirits can be called demons or devils, enemies of man that need to be placated or deceived by horrifying rituals and taboos. But animism need not be negative. Actually, the basic idea behind animism makes a kind of ecological sense. Humans are part of a living web of interconnections. There have been some successful and benign ecological adaptations, such as the bushmen of the Kalahari Desert, but unfortunately these are being wiped out—"extincted"—by the spread of Western Civilization, with its web-destroying economic interests. The new concept of "Gaia," the name used for "Earth, as a single living organism," is a sort of up-to-date form of animism and has much to recommend it.

Joseph Campbell tells all about the evolution of animism in the first of his four-volume work, *The Masks of God*. The development went in two directions, depending on the livelihood of the human group.

Hunters concentrated on the animal spirits. They saw themselves related to those spirits, descended from them somehow. Their main concern was to secure permission from the spirits to use the bodies of the animals they hunted and killed, and to guarantee that the spirits would continue to provide more animal bodies for their use. The totem-spirits were then enlisted to help with the hunt itself. The humans sensed their relatedness to the animals.

Human groups who "advanced" to farming had other worries, like the weather and soil preparation. A major concern came from the observation that the seed had to die in order to sprout and multiply. Ritualistic means of guaranteeing that dying and multiplying process were invented, with sacrifice at the root of it. Sometimes it was a symbolic dying, but often ritualistic slaughters took place.

At this stage, both groups of humans conceived of these animating spirits as gods and goddesses. The deer god. The corn goddess. The sun god. The rain god. The river goddess. To guarantee the continuation of their way of life, people had to deal with all these gods. This stage is called polytheism.

From here, we can pick up the history of "God" from the Bible. The historical sections of the book of Genesis begin at the time of Abraham. Abraham's family were polytheists. He became a deviant by deciding to practice monolatry. That is, he was going to worship one God only—YHWH. YHWH became the tribal god of the extended family of Abraham. YHWH took care of the nomad flocks, the pastures and the wells, the fertility of ewes and women, taboos about diet and sexual behavior, and laws about slavery and inheritance. Social control, within the tribe, was a religious matter, and still is in many parts of the world.

Each tribe had its own gods. The Abrahamites had theirs, but there was only one. They didn't necessarily deny the existence of the gods of the other tribes, with their different names and different taboos and commandments. They ignored them, or scorned them, out of loyalty to YHWH. In fact, YHWH admitted to being jealous and, according to the priests and prophets, became nasty whenever any of his people tried worshipping other gods. The descendants of Abraham's grandson, Israel, seem to have invented the idea that YHWH became involved in human history. At least they take credit for it. Not only hunting and agriculture, but historical developments are also YHWH's concerns, they said.

The most drastic and alarming historical activity, so far, had been war and conquest. So YHWH became a war god. He brought his people out of Egypt, defeated the Egyptian pursuers, whipped the Amalekites and others, fought for and with his people in the conquest of Canaan, and promised to drive out the Canaanites, the Hittites, the Hivites, the Perrizites, the Girgashites, the Amorites and the Jebusites. But, since the Israelites did not complete mopping-up operations, supposedly because of their fascination for those other gods, YHWH did not drive all the foreigners out of Canaan, but left them there to "test" Israel. The twelve tribes lived in something very much like anarchy for a while. "In those days there was no king in Israel, and everyman did what was right in his own eyes."

There was a fatal interest in the gods of the Canaanites, which can be accounted for. The nomad Israelites were herdsmen and plunderers. The Canaanites were farmers. The technology of farming included the worship of the Baals, the localized fertility gods. Their worship included human sacrifice, but also some rather sexy behavior, which no doubt helped arouse the interest of the newcomers. Besides, hunters who are going to learn how to grow grain need all the technological assistance they can get. Better check out this temple prostitution business, and these local ceremonies "on every high hill and under every green tree." The judges and the prophets of the Hebrews raged against this corruption of YHWH-worship. Yet in the end, YHWH had to become versatile enough to be a fertility god himself—how else would the grain grow for the Israelites?

Meanwhile, YHWH helped get a central government organized, choosing Saul as king, then rejecting him in favor of David. YHWH's exploits as a war god helped put together a large empire for David and his son, Solomon. Then YHWH permitted the splitting away of most of the empire from Solomon's son, leaving two nations with the same god, YHWH.

The larger non-Davidic nation was swallowed up by Assyria a couple of centuries later. This development was accounted for by saying that YHWH gave up the struggle to win them away from idolatry. They became the "ten lost tribes"—but they weren't lost in the sense that they could turn up later in Great Britain or Utah—they were lost in the sense that they were deported to Nineveh and absorbed into the population there and exterminated as a separately identifiable people. The Samaritans descended from those that weren't deported, who mixed with new settlers.

Meanwhile, YHWH, as a jealous war god, was in trouble. All he had left was a tiny state called Judah—Jerusalem and its rocky suburbs and little more—under threat from both Assyria and Egypt. Not much for a war god to be proud of. Judah was finally overwhelmed by Nebuchadnezzar, king of the Mesopotamian Empire of Babylon. The Jews, as they were called by then, went into exile.

This was a very important crisis for YHWH. The world almost lost him at this point. But some strange notions were invented, which saved him. Some of the earlier prophets had laid down important groundwork, and the prophets of the exile completed the task.

YHWH was active in history all right, but not as a divine secret war weapon of the Jews. YHWH became identified with certain abstract ideals, like Truth and Justice. Because of injustice, not religious jealousy, YHWH could change sides, and fight on the side of Nebuchadnezzar *against* his people in Jerusalem, to punish them and teach them. Amos, Hosea and Jeremiah said this most clearly. Second Isaiah and Ezekiel clarified it further, in exile.

YHWH is invisible. YHWH cares more about social justice, kindness, mercy and truthfulness than the temple and its priests or religious rituals. He destroyed his own temple to prove it. Now in exile in Babylon, the Jews discover that YHWH isn't confined to the land of Canaan. He is not a local tribal war god. YHWH is present in Babylon, too. YHWH is even present over in Persia. Their new king, Cyrus, has been put into position by YHWH, in order to arrange for the Jews' return home later.

YHWH is everywhere. YHWH made everything, and rules over it. YHWH is the only god there is. He is the Creator of all things, the heavens and the earth. The whole earth is his, the world and they that dwell therein. He loves all people. He chose the Jews to be his special suffering servant people, to be the agents and channels of his intent to bless the whole world.

This is monotheism. There *is* only one God. The Jews know who he is. They know his name—YHWH. By this time he also goes by the generic name, "God," and will henceforth. He is a supporter of justice, because he is just. He can be stern, but he dislikes indiscriminate violence. He chose the Jews, say the prophets, for reasons that are inexplicable, to be instruments of his purpose to do good to all. He is not anyone's secret weapon against the rest. No people are his favorites, but he has special tasks for the Jews. So, we now have one invisible God, a chosen, but not favorite people, and a world full of violence and misery, especially where the large empires keep expanding and contracting through ceaseless warring and destruction.

A couple of centuries go by—characterized by violent imperial musical chairs: Babylon, Persia, Greece, Rome. It seems hopeless. The Jews are kept going by a strange hope for a God-sent Deliverer/Messiah, who many are sure will have an anti-imperial political/military mission.

Among the other peoples of that time and place—Greeks, Persians, Syrians, Egyptians, Romans—thoughtful, sensitive persons give up on the world in large numbers. Mystery religions arise, all very similar. The general description of them all will sound very familiar. A young god/hero, born of a virgin, lives an exemplary and miracle-filled but short human life, and dies unjustly. He rises again from the dead, and lets his followers in on the secret of eternal life, beyond death. He becomes their savior from sin and physical limitations. As the world goes to final total ruin, he rescues his followers and joins them to himself in eternal otherworldly bliss. For some the savior's name was Attis, for others it was Mithra, and there were several more of these mystery religions.

In the early decades of the Roman Empire, a new mystery religion arose in the Near East and spread to Greece and Rome. This new one built on that history of "God" that we have been tracing from Abraham. A Jewish prophet/rabbi, Jesus of Nazareth, was lynched with tacit but illegal Roman approval. He was declared Messiah, Son of God, and resurrected Savior, and worshipped as a Divine Being.

Most of the Jews regarded and still regard that as a step backward. The One invisible God cannot have a Son—he is not *that* kind of fertility god—and YHWH has not turned his back permanently on the world he has created. But the Christians interpret the suffering servant passages of Isaiah's writings to refer to Jesus, the Savior, not to Israel as a people, nor to the Christians as the new Israel. The blessing God has for the whole world is the Good News that the God/Savior of the Christians will save them, too, if they submit to him.

For several centuries it was not certain which of several of these popular and very similar mystery religions would win the day. The Roman Emperor Constantine, in the fourth century, made sure that it was the "God" of the Christians to whom all the world must someday submit. That prepared the scene for missionaries and fresh new empires, and popes who can lock people they don't like out of Heaven. It led to Inquisitions and Crusades and unbelievable slaughter in the name of Peace and Love. It made possible Christian rulers capable of believing that they are God's chosen instruments for the punishment and destruction of whole peoples, and now recently of the very planet itself, if need be. All in the name of "God."

For many centuries thinking about "God" was placed in the hands of specialists, and left there. Theologians they were called, and non-theologians were not supposed to think about the big questions, such as "Is there a God?" or "What is God like?" The rank and file were simply expected to obey.

Theologians came and went, and over the ages schools of them could be identified, based partly on the accidents of history and partly on the contents of the books the theologians wrote. "Oh, that's Augustinian." "Oh, that's Thomistic," for Thomas Aquinas. "Oh, that's Calvinism."

Thomas, in the 13th century, attempted the great feat of summarizing all there was to know about God, including logical proofs of his existence and detailed statements as to his nature and purpose. He built a great theological system, which still stands as authoritative for Roman Catholics and is quite impressive. John Calvin, in the 16th century, built a similar system for the Protestant Reformation.

"Systematic Theology" is still the name of the most prestigious department in seminaries, and it consists of three main branches: The Doctrine of God and Creation, The Doctrine of Christ and the Atonement and The Doctrine of the Church.

Systematic theology? Can God be put into a logical system? Is God a system? The questions Systematic Theology deals with seem far removed from the life most people are living, and sometimes the logical and theological answers verge on the absurd or the immoral.

For example, one theologian stated that, based on his theological premises, it would be possible for Adolf Eichman to go to heaven if only he would accept Jesus Christ as his personal Lord and Savior in time, before the Israelis hanged him, but that it would not be possible for any of the six million Jews that Eichman murdered to do so, since they *were* Jews, that is, *not* believers in Jesus Christ. That kind of thinking is repulsive to me, and besides, I think we have a right to question the relevance of the exaggerated concern about "going to heaven."

People have other, real problems to deal with: floundering marriages, alcoholism, petty gossip, hunger, birth, funerals for sixteen-year-olds, ninety-year-old vegetables who linger on, war, despair. Systematic Theology makes assertions that don't have to do with anything important.

But some theologians started the process of questioning "God." Many of them have been labeled heretics by the official churches that made them into God specialists, that is, theologians. And some non-heretics also advanced the process, which must be included as part of my history of "God."

Karl Barth wrote his 20th century version of systematic theology, and made some startling assertions, such as, "Christianity is not a religion." What? Of course it is. When you read Barth carefully, you can spot his awareness that the religions of man have been studied by sociologists and found to have two main functions: (1) grant divine sanction for whatever the social group is doing, and (2) placate the numinous, which means, "get the unseen Powers That Be off our backs." Barth thinks that Christianity doesn't do that. That's why he says Christianity is not a religion. It is Truth, he says, final revelation from "God" as to *how it is*. Barth also referred to "the God who really *is* God," as if to say that when some people use the word "God," they are not referring to the "real God," that is, the one that Barth's referring to.

Rudolph Bultmann asked Barth to state his preconceptions. Barth was puzzled. "I have none. I'm just telling you how it is." It verges on the comical. No human being can function at all without his own perspective and preconceived notions, but Barth couldn't spot his own.

Bultmann, it turns out, was *really* questioning "God." He admitted that he was ready and willing, and even eager, to bring Christianity into line with modern scientific thought by tossing out every instance of what he called "interventionist myth." A lot was stripped away in so doing.

Imagine that the world is like a toy ant farm. God is the boy who owns the ant farm. The ants go about their business, doing their thing, marching two by two, digging tunnels, eating, laying eggs, all that. The boy, from time to time, reaches in and pokes into the ant farm with a stick, breaking up tunnels, disturbing eggs, crushing individual ants. "I'm gonna get *that* ant!" Smasho!

Bultmann says that's not the way it is. God does not, or maybe cannot, interfere like that. The story of the parting of the Red Sea to save the Israelites, for example, is a case of interventionist myth.

Bill Cosby summarized the idea perfectly in his routine on Noah, when Noah asked God to change one of the two female hippos he had brought in, to save his having to go hunt for a male. God replied—correctly, Bultmann would have added—"You know I don't work like that." This notion is quite important. Can God interfere, for whatever reason? Is there such a God? But if God doesn't interfere, big chunks of the Bible and tradition go by the board.

Dietrich Bonhoeffer wrote non-systematic theology from his cell in a Nazi prison. He lamented the fact that we think of God as a stopgap, mainly. Whenever we're stuck, we bring God in. Otherwise we don't need him or bother with him much. As the circle of our knowledge widens, we push God further and further away, out on the outer rim of an ever-enlarging circle, farther and farther away, less and less relevant to our daily lives. For the most part, we can get along without God.

Paul Tillich used a phrase to describe God—"The Ground of Our Being." His thought was widely rejected, by those who bothered to try to understand it, as "oriental," which it is. "Pantheistic" it was also called, which it also is, in a way. The Ground of Our Being was too big a mental jump for most Christians, including the theologians.

Nothing less than the existence of God was at stake in all this. It was an old question. "Does God exist?" "Exist" means "to be outside." "To be," but in the sense of "to be, as over against something else." But God, Tillich said, is the Source of all existence. Things exist because of God, maybe. God is the ground of existence. But "God," as an entity, does not exist. It would have been a bombshell, if it had been allowed to go off, but most folks heard only another dud. "Theologians don't make sense." But this one *does* make sense. If "God" exists, outside of this existence that we are in, where is he? Where does he hang out? "Truly, thou art a God that hidest thyself," lamented one of the old prophets.

Bishop James Robinson came along with a book called *Honest To God*. Bishops aren't supposed to admit that they doubt or question the formulae of systematic theology, but this one did. He did his doubting in print, and then asserted flatly that there was no God "up there." The old Biblical and medieval three-story universe of Heaven, Earth, and Hell, isn't there. There's no such thing. But the bishop went on. In our Copernican universe, there is no God "out there," either. Oh-oh.

Where is he, then? Where shall we look? Look "down here," Robinson said. Look "in there." Within yourself, and in the human connections you find yourself in the middle of. He was trying to understand Tillich's idea, "The Ground of Our Being," but that leads inevitably to pantheism, orientalism, alchemy and heresy.

Where is God? What kind of God is there? Where do the important things come from—things like life, love, faith, justice, longing, hope? Are they dreams that die at dawn? Is there any Ground, any Basis, for them? Why should we cast our life in with them? Is there nothing to do and nothing to hope for but a quick grab at—at what?—before it's all gone?

We need to be aware of anthropomorphism. We humans have fashioned "God" in our own image. We couldn't help it, being human. In the Bible, especially in the early sections, God is extremely humanoid. He takes afternoon strolls in the Garden of Eden in the cool of the day. He has hands, and fingers, and feet, and a footstool, and a face. Moses got to see his backside, it says. God has feelings, like anger and jealousy and grief and vengefulness. He has a will, a plan.

Here we are, trying to think of the Source of Cosmic Being, the Original Void, the Unmade Uncaused Cause, the Root of Power, Justice and Love in all the galaxies—and we're stuck with images that suggest that all that is a glorified human being! Probably we can't help it. Maybe we have to do that. But at least we could admit we're doing it! Perhaps "God" is really a figure of speech, for all that Source stuff. Every attribute we assign to him/her/it is *our* doing. Reality is surely something else.

The Hebrew prophets railed against idols and idolatry. For some of them "idols" referred to "the gods of the nations," meaning simply other people's gods. Other prophets said enough to enable us to define idolatry more carefully. "The work of men's hands," was a favorite description—some extension of ourselves, some entity that we invented and which belongs to us as a group, and not to everyone. The prophets attacked idols from several different angles, mocking them as unreal, powerless, deaf, empty, inert, dead. "There was no voice; no one answered." "They have eyes but they see not, ears but they hear not; noses have they, but they smell not."

The Baals of the Canaanites were essentially fertility gods. Their worship included temple prostitution and sacrifice of the fruit that agriculture and animal husbandry produced.

Moloch and Chemosh were gods of the Moabites and Ammonites, very similar, both dedicated to cruelty. Human sacrifice was commonly offered to placate those idols. Whenever Israelites allowed their children to be offered up, the prophets were furious. It happened, because humans are willing to do terrible things with the hope of gaining some kind of cosmic insurance.

Mammon was the name of the god of financial profit. The worship of this idol has not been stamped out. In our time the profit motive is closely linked to the cult of cruelty. Variations on this form of idolatry are nearly endless. Children, rain forests, rivers, beaches, dolphins, rainfall itself and the ozone layer have all been sacrificed on the altar of Mammon, even though we no longer call it that.

The invention of monotheism should have clarified things a good bit, but it didn't. It should have been obvious that it's no longer a case of one god versus others. There is only one. So either you're dealing with the only one there is, or you're dealing with an idol. If your deity isn't the deity for The Whole Thing, you have an idol. It seems simple, but as it turned out in practical terms, "idolatry" became simply a term useful for knocking down other people's belief systems. The universal implications of monotheism are easily lost sight of. And when one's own system is called idolatry, great indignation results.

Nineteen hundred years ago, the most popular idol was called "Roma." Later it was called "Hispania" in one area and "Francia" in another and "Brittania" in yet another. In the name of that imperial idol, great quantities of murder and enslavement and arson and theft took place. All of that was excused with explanations of "civilizing responsibilities" and "the white man's burden" and "the spread of the message of the Prince of Peace and his salvation."

In our day and place this same most popular idol could be called AMERICA, but our arrogance has carried us on beyond such obvious nationalistic idolatry. We have deceived ourselves as a result. Our idol is called simply "God." That generic term makes it so simple, so slick. The idea that the only "God" that exists is somehow *ours* is idolatry. It is obvious, really, yet so hard for some folks to spot.

There are some popular non-Biblical proverbs that show how this name change works. "This is God's country" combined with "My country, right or wrong." Here you have the old imperial idol firmly in place. "God helps those who help themselves." Here you have the old Mammon-worship installed, stronger than ever because it isn't recognized as idolatry. For these idol-worshippers, God is an American. Some go so far as to believe, and even say, that God is a Republican. He has his priests and prophets, too, for "God and country."

God is a major participant in our national Holy Days. Proud, smug prayers accentuate the celebration of Independence Day. God helped found this country in the wilderness, we're told. The people who were already here, with their established civilizations, didn't count, except as part of the fauna—wild beasts that had to be exterminated, towns and granaries and all. Treaties with them did not require truthfulness of word or intent. This same cynicism carries over into current "national security" uses of assassination, double agents, deception and diplomacy—all necessary aspects of

Prophet With No God

the conflicts we get into in the name of "God."

The establishment of a fair number of the original colonies was a religious enterprise—Massachusetts for the Pilgrims and the Puritans, Rhode Island for the Dissenters, Pennsylvania for the Quakers, Maryland for the Roman Catholics. When it came time to amalgamate the colonies, all the religious disagreement was swallowed up in the new American idolatry.

Thanksgiving Day was set aside to offer thanks for the special protection the deity gives—not to humanity, or to Planet Earth—but to newly arrived land-grabbing white "Americans," and it included thanks for plagues that were wiping out entire native tribes, whose land the invaders were stealing.

Memorial Day was designed to commemorate the war dead, and to continue to justify the bloody history of the nation.

Armistice Day was originally observed to note the end of the war to end wars, but it no longer rings true, what with Franco and Tojo and Hitler and Stalin and Korea and Vietnam and Nicaragua and Kuwait. So—watch this!—Armistice Day has been converted into a confusing batch of Holy Days, all called Veterans Day, when we honor the soldiers! Not the end of war at all, but the perpetuation of it, and an obscene war budget to go with it. We shouldn't let ourselves be fooled by the label "defense."

The American war god is named "God." It's a brilliant trick. If he were called Mars or Ares or Bechtel or something like that, this clarification would not be necessary. Even Mother's Day is part of the idolatry, because it honors American mothers only. Otherwise we'd hear more about the mothers of the *desaparecidos* all over Latin America, the mothers of famine in Africa, the mothers of Cambodia and Vietnam and Poland and Palestine and Iran and Iraq.

All this can be correctly labeled idolatry, because the "God" applies only to a part, not the whole. Any time the deity is the god of some portion, partiality results, and that's idolatry.

The worship of the American war god flies in the face of the implications of monotheism. If there is only one God, he can't be ours. He can't be anybody's. There's only one, for all. He alone has to be enough for everybody. He has to be the God of the Poles, the Nicaraguans, the Ethiopians, the Mohicans, the Aztecs, the Chinese, the Soviets, whether they believe in him or not, the Iranians, no matter how fanatical their beliefs are—everybody. How many Gods are there? One, or more than one?

Lincoln saw that at the time of our Civil War. People on both sides prayed to "God" for victory. Was there a northern God and a southern God? What was the one God, for both, supposed to do? In his second inaugural address, Lincoln, like the old Hebrew prophets before him, turned to abstract justice for his explanation:

"The Almighty has his own purposes ... Fondly do we hope, fervently do we pray, that this mighty scourge of war may speedily pass away. Yet, if God wills that it continue until all the wealth piled by the bond-man's two hundred and fifty years of unrequited toil shall be sunk, and until every drop of blood drawn with the lash shall be paid by another drawn with the sword, as was said three thousand years ago, so still it must be said, that the judgments of the Lord are true and righteous altogether."

Partisans of American military nationalism don't think like that. They think America is first and best, and they assume that "God" thinks so, too. Precisely that indicates the idolatry. They think of the planet as something America can take, by purchase or conquest or "cultural influence." They hate the people who thwart us and try to kick us out.

Nationalism is a very dangerous plague which infects this whole planet and needs to be eradicated. "God" will probably not be much help, because the label, at least for the time being, has been captured by those who think in terms of parts only, not the whole.

One god for the whole planet might be a good idea, for now. Intergalactic communication will necessitate further growth in the evolution of the concept. But for the time being, such a notion

Prophet With No God 147

would amount to a huge leap, or an arduous uphill task, just to symbolize for people one human species and one endangered planet. Some of us don't want the whales left out!

A friend who was about to join Alcoholics Anonymous wrote to me about her quandary concerning "the higher power." I called and told her that my philosophy was more and more *not* to rely on some other force, real or imaginary, "out there." The task was within, I said. "That won't do for an alcoholic," she replied, and asked me to write out my belief system. So I tried:

I must begin with negations, as the Hindus and the Buddhists do. I do not believe that the Universe is an artifact, a thing made by some other thing, who isn't part of it but can nevertheless interfere in it. The Universe is what it is, it is constructed the way it is, out of itself by development of itself. It is what there is, all there is. And it is intelligent—it has produced us! It has will and plan, and expresses itself through us. It is perfectly interconnected, and so are we, much more so than the illusion created by our separated bodies seems to indicate. I suspect that the Basic Stuff of the universe is mental and that Mind expresses itself in bodies in the physical world. That makes me a Mentalist, or a philosophical Idealist, if we need labels.

"God," as used by AA and churches, will not do for me. "God" is a code-word, a metaphor for Everything-there-is-the-way-it-is. I seldom use that code-word because almost everyone else means something else, which I know I don't believe in. The Higher Self which is within and which is not the ego, the True Self, the Self of the World, the Whole Thing, What-there-is-the-way-it-is, It—with a lot of *um* and *er* and *uh* and *om* and *I'm-not-sure-just-how-to-put-this* and *I-don't-have-the-words*—It is really there. That is, here. Here we are. It is. But It is not apart from what there is. It is what there is. It is quite marvelous and *Om* is the correct response.

All of that is within. Within me and within you and everyone else, and everything else. Our faculty of consciousness—which not everyone uses very much, but the capacity for it is there—makes us special among the beings we are in contact with. It also makes the dolphins and whales special. Within an infinite universe, anything is possible, even likely, it seems to me.

Letting one's thought drift in this direction makes one's head spin. Meanwhile we have life to live. I believe the Universe is, and does what it does, and is arranged the way it is. I do not yet comprehend very much of it, comparing by percentages what *is* with what I know. Yet I find I can trust It. I am somehow an embodiment of It, an expression of It. So are you. It doesn't need for you to drink anymore. She, or It through you, has learned whatever that "lesson" contained. So you quit, and you and It can get on with other lessons.

I suspect that AA and "going back to church" must feel like a step backward for you. It would for me. I battled my father continually over it. He used to think that I'd forgotten something and he wanted to remind me of it, some verse or text or theological point. I told him I've forgotten nothing, nothing at all, that I've moved on.

The English word "God" is hard to pronounce. Exactly which "o" sound do we want? Check how you pronounce it in the plural, "the gods of the nations are idols..." Now try the singular, and capitalize it, and use it to refer to the Source of Power and Justice and Love in the Cosmos. Or use it to refer to the little tin-horn deity you keep in your pocket for emergencies and to underwrite your cosmic fire insurance, which you're pretty sure you won't be needing for quite a while yet. It makes a difference how you pronounce it. I noticed this in seminary, and have kept my ears on it every since.

For myself, I wanted "God" to rhyme with "broad"—a little

more "o" than rhyming with "sod," which was the standard dictionary designation. I was trying to sound more like a Hebrew prophet—"God is not to be trifled with," "God is not on our side for sure," "God is not mocked," "Prepare to meet your God...!"

There were others further out than I, who made "God" rhyme with "load." They sounded threatening, and never mentioned Divine Love, except to terrify people, reconciling it somehow with a belief in Wrath and Hell. I didn't want to be one of them, wasn't one of them, and left fundamentalism early on because of that mean streak I had noticed.

But others flattened that "o" almost to an "a," making "God" rhyme with "sad." This God was your pal, easy to get along with, easier to fool than Santa Claus. I found him quite disgusting early on, and still do. This is the god of those TV evangelists, who grow wealthy on the gifts of the gullible, and of some "New Age" sorts, who want you to think life is an easy ride and especially want you to make it one for them.

In the end, I had to toss out all of these "Gods" and all these pronunciations. I could envy the superstitious Jews of old who wouldn't pronounce The Name at all. They honored the name too much to risk mispronouncing it. I'm ready to eschew the name now, in order to avoid confusion.

"God" did not create the world. No Entity did. It simply is. I suspect the cosmos is eternal and infinite, without a beginning. I suspect that existence is circular, not linear. So we don't need the name, and don't need to pronounce it.

Dualism is the belief that everything is divided between Good and Evil, that all of existence is an endless war between Good and Evil. Christianity, in theory, is not supposed to be dualistic. God made everything, they say, including the Devil, and even the bad things that happen are somehow God's doing. This notion turns up in some Old Testament prophets and in the story of the Exodus, where "God hardened the heart of Pharaoh." It is also in the notion that God arranged the crucifixion of Jesus in order to save the world.

In the Book of Revelation, the cosmic war between Good and Evil is concluded and the Devil is defeated and cast into the lake of fire. But this is really a form of Dualism, in which Good "wins," which is illogical. What happens next? Notice that the Devil is not destroyed, and not won back, and not recognized as the other side of a single coin. He remains eternally evil, which is still Dualism, and the conflict goes on forever.

The theoretical attempts of Christian theologians to get beyond Dualism have been weak and unconvincing, and popular Christianity has been blatantly dualistic. "God votes for you, and the Devil votes against you, and you cast the deciding vote."

It's interesting to see what happens when you catch yourself no longer believing in something. I gave up believing in demons, and the Devil, fairly soon after I began to be really thoughtful about these things. No good God would allow any being, human or devil, to suffer "eternal conscious torment." But like everyone else I had been believing in a form of Dualism, and you can't have half of Dualism. If you give up one half of the belief system, and keep thinking, the other half is in trouble. It took a while, but I finally concluded that "God" likewise had to go.

Later, I found Monism. Monism is not half of Dualism, the way one is half of two. Monism comes from a different view of evil, and of values, and of change. Monism says there is only One Thing. It is a step beyond monotheism, which says there is only one God. Monism says there is only one, at all, altogether. All things are parts of One. When Chinese philosophy refers to The Ten Thousand Things, it means all this many-ness, subsumed under The One. There is only One. There is One.

You may, but you don't need to, call The All, or The One, "God." I would say that it's not a good idea to do so, because of all

Prophet With No God 151

the erroneous dualistic baggage that word drags into our thinking. Dualism is derived from ego. Good and Evil are perceived and defined and distinguished by their effect on ego. Monism goes beyond ego, beyond Good and Evil, to the overarching One-ness of The Whole Thing. Monism, finally, leaves ego behind, and that's good riddance.

In exile the Jews learned that God was not tied to the landmass of Jerusalem, and thus they invented monotheism. In my career failure and its aftermath, I learned that "God" was not confined to the church, and then I learned that as a secret weapon, as an Entity that could rescue me, God wasn't there at all. *That* "God" was an idol, a broken idol.

I found Monism, The All, The Undeviating Justice, and my ego was terrified. I survived that, but "God" didn't.

And then I began noticing clues—I could call them messengers—the old word was "angels." They came in strange forms. Old friends. New friends. Strange books. Birds. A parakeet taught me to quit pushing the wheel so much, a habit left over from the old days of trying to "do the will of God." A mockingbird taught me to do my thing—his is singing!—without so much concern about who's listening or who cares.

A friend of mine takes angels quite literally—entities that live mostly in another realm, another dimension, another mode of manifestation, but that can get into ours enough to make contact. Something stirred the windowful of mobiles in her apartment, and I didn't think it was simply the wind. The window was closed. Messengers, she thinks they are. Angels.

Another friend tells frankly and flatly of being accosted by what he calls "entities" who are not terrestrial beings at all. He tests them, and they pass his reality tests to his satisfaction. They seem to be recruiting him for something they're up to. They haven't recruited me at all, either directly or through him. But he is not psychotic, so I have to allow room in my own "belief system" for—something.

Not "God." I am now convinced that that was an idol. I took part in that idol worship, and now I do not. But in an infinite universe, all things are possible. Things I cannot imagine are possible, even downright likely. So, I'm trying to be open as much as my limited little experience and limited little analytical mind and limited little powers of imagination will allow. I haven't thought of everything. I don't know for sure what is and what isn't, what exists and what doesn't. More things are possible than I'm capable of dreaming of.

That's why I don't call myself an atheist. *That* God isn't there. But how do I know what all *is* there, somewhere, somehow? It seems illogical to make sweeping negative statements. Just because I've never met a ghost, that I know of, doesn't prove anything definitively. The mechanistic determinists, sometimes called scientists, are in error in declaring that what they cannot perceive and measure *isn't there*. How do they know?

It seems downright likely that intelligent live beings that are not human or physical like us, exist. It is not utterly preposterous that they and we could interact in some way. It is not unlikely that they are more intelligent than we in many ways. I am trying to stay open.

The portion of the cosmos that the humans have examined is minuscule. The portion that the humans fully understand of what they have examined is minuscule again. There are at least as many galaxies as there are suns in our galaxy. For us to see it now, the light from the nearest galaxy left there before there were any humans on earth. The possibilities in a cosmos like that are beyond imagining. We are free to imagine anything, and not free to be certain about very much.

I must note one more thing before leaving this "God" and messenger business. I don't pretend to know where it comes from, but there is a spirit that keeps popping up in human affairs that will not be defeated, no matter how often it is beaten down or corrupted and overcome. It keeps rearing up in some form of minority protest. The Powers That Be crush it, but it will not die and stay dead. Or, The Powers That Be absorb it and it changes sides and peters out, but only temporarily.

St. Francis of Assisi. Santa Teresa of Avila. They were made saints so that no one would take seriously what they said. John Hus. They burned him at the stake. Martin Luther. He became part of a new Establishment after the monolithic Catholic medieval unity broke apart, and the spirit was dissipated. John Calvin. The spirit couldn't handle political and economic power and fizzled out. The Quakers. The Mennonites. The Methodists. Again, absorption into the Establishment frittered away the newness, the freshness, the truth.

Luddites. Universalists. New Age, One World Peace Activists. Flower Children. Organic Gardening advocates. Equality agitators. Health nuts. Greens. Over and over this spirit—for all I can tell, the same one—appears and makes much the same point afresh. The Powers That Be crush it, if they can. Or they make it part of their established power system, which does away with that fresh message. The Ogre Holdfast kills the Hero. But that spirit will rise again. What is this thing I'm calling a spirit? I don't know. But I believe in it, and I try to stay open to it, and get in touch with it, whenever I see it. It's strange having no name for it, not knowing where it will turn up next, not even knowing what it is.

26. HUMAN NATURE

Christian doctrine teaches that there is something wrong with human nature. Old myths that tell about primordial disobedience have been drilled into our collective unconscious minds. Many individuals, including me, found childhood completely spoiled by the incessant message that we are bad, something is wrong with us, we have done bad deeds and left undone what was expected of us. The resulting sense of guilt becomes a habit of mind very hard to break. "Old tapes play in our heads," many therapists have noted. They haven't yet devised quick and easy ways to dismantle the mechanism that plays those tapes. "You are a bad boy!" "You messed up that one, per usual." "You deserve the bad things that are happening or are about to happen to you."

The Christians call this the Doctrine of Sin. The hierarchical arrangement of different acts, or sins, according to the degree of seriousness always seemed silly to me. Luther and Calvin got to me early. Everything you do, every thought you have, every breath you take—it is all sin, because you are a sinner, and you can't make up for it by doing penance, praying, or going to church. It is hopeless, because you are hopeless.

Of course, the Christian answer to all this is grace and forgiveness, but I have noted how few really do believe in this. Those who do believe it tend to become disgustingly smug. "I'm saved. Are you saved?" "I'm ready to die and go and be with God. Are you ready?" They're really not much fun to be around.

But the vast majority do not really believe in grace. The most startling instance of that, for me, was my father. He was dying and he looked afraid. I told him so. "Of course, I'm afraid!" he said, looking surprised as well as very scared.

"How can you be afraid, after all that you taught us about God and Jesus and forgiveness and heaven and all that?"

He snorted and shook his head "no," which meant, as always, "Now we're through talking about that!"

He only half-believed what he had taught me. He was guilty and he knew it. Not of violence and warmongering, but of things left undone, mostly. Life left unlived. He was not smug. He was afraid. God will judge, and soon now, he thought. He had been depending on the easy answers of conservative Christianity and, when his own case became immediate and unavoidable, they let him down.

I have come to believe that the Christian doctrine of forgiveness is a bad idea. If it's true that some are forgiven by "God" for their misdeeds of commission and omission, on the basis of their assent to some creedal formulation, then the Cosmos is immoral. I'm convinced such teaching is simply part of an ecclesiastical racket. "Pay here, and we'll arrange forgiveness for you." Tetzel was doing it with his indulgences in medieval Germany. Martin Luther had the last word on the topic even then, it seems to me: "If the Pope really can free souls from Purgatory, if he can arrange, or hurry up, that forgiveness process, then why does he not do so, for love's sake?" What does money have to do with it? If you can buy forgiveness, it isn't forgiveness at all. I have little difficulty dismissing this doctrine as erroneous and immoral.

There are unavoidable times when we injure or offend one another. "Forgive and forget," someone will tell you, as if that would get rid of the rancor in your heart. It is remarkable how often we are instructed to forget. I do not believe forgetting can be commanded. And forgiveness that is a response to a command is not forgiveness at all.

Parents try this with their children. "Forgive your brother!" Something that an unaware person might call "peace" may be restored temporarily, but rancor does not go away in that manner. Grown siblings seldom get along well, I've noticed, and that may be partly why. Forgiveness was injected by force, and didn't work. If I had it all to do over, I think I would simply say, as parent, in such a crisis, "You may have done permanent damage to your relationship with your brother. Is that your intention? What is this fight really all about?" I never ever said, "Forgive and forget," to my children, although it was said to me when I was a child.

Forgiveness is too easy, too glib, too shallow. I'm not sure there is such a thing at all. It looks like a word used to refer to a cover-up, not a real resolution. People near me call me an elephant. "He never forgets." Actually it's not true. I can forget, and do. I have even done some very deliberate erasing of people and situations I'm done with—I find I can put them out of my mind and I have done so. But it is not forgiveness. It is a hostile act. I am closing off contact, defending myself.

We have family members, grown siblings, who seem to think that the passage of a lot of time indicates that forgiveness has occurred, even though not a word has been said. I mean not a word of apology, nor any kind of admission of ignorance or lack of awareness. But since it was ten or twenty years ago—destructive malicious gossip, theft, whatever—it's OK now to resume cordial relations as if nothing had happened. I'm not good at it, and on that account am called an elephant, as if remembering was bad. Again, at my age, I'm told to forgive and forget. I end up suspecting that there is no such thing as forgiveness at all. And I've seen situations in which the pretense that everything is now all right festers and poisons and becomes literally life-threatening. No, *truth* is better than forgiveness.

Pardons have completely fouled up our so-called system of penal justice. I have devised a plan that would completely rearrange that system. Motivation would have nothing to do with anything. And of course, neither would relationships with judges and governors and presidents. What happened would be the only question. The one who injured someone else would be made to repay the injured party in one way or another. Prisons would be only for the criminally insane, and everyone in there would be in for life. No pardons, political or other. For all the rest, on the outside, repayment would be the issue. Recompense would be required, no matter how long it took.

In the near future all our business will be conducted by means of ID cards and a central computer. Cash transactions are already difficult, even cash deposits from a large number of small transactions. My reformed penal system would consist simply of

ascertaining who caused injury to whom, and how much the all-wise judge or jury determined it was worth. Enter it into the computer and re-total the new balances. Prison would be accounting, not guards and razor ribbon and schools for crime.
There's a sense in which real life is like that, I think. We may have the illusion that we're getting away with something, but we are not. Some kind of record is being kept—in the rocks, in the brains. "There is nothing secret that shall not be made known." "What shall it profit a man, if he gain the whole world, and lose his own soul?" "Woe to that man by whom the offense cometh." "He to whom much is given, of him shall much be required." "There shall be weeping and gnashing of teeth." "You will never get out until you have paid the last penny."

Having disposed of forgiveness, what about sin? I don't use the word anymore. I let the ecclesiastical racketeers have it. But the idea that something is the matter with the humans won't go away—not with the world situation, and many a personal situation, in such a mess.

Some would say that humans are much less intelligent than they think they are. Stupidity is the problem. Not ignorance, for which information could be a simple solution. No, it's stupidity—collective stupidity, especially—a kind of inability to apply reasoning to the most urgent problems that confront humanity. Groups are stupider than individuals, and the problems will have to be solved by groups, or not at all. Individuals can't do it. I cannot repair the ozone layer. I cannot dispose of nuclear waste safely. The group will have to, and the prospects that the group really will are not good.

Besides this denseness when it comes to collective problem-solving, there seem to be other flaws in human nature. Violent behavior that may have had a survival value in the days of saber-toothed tigers is inappropriate now. The way humans can turn that violence on each other nowadays must be regarded as a flaw. And the way humans in positions of power can decry the use of violence on a small scale while they prepare for and use violence on a huge scale is a serious flaw.

Most humans have a self-excusing tendency which can be downright comical. "It fell." "It broke." "The woman whom thou gavest to me to be with me did beguile me and I did eat." "It's not my fault." "I was only obeying orders." "I don't know what got into me."

In not every case, but upon careful examination, one must say in a remarkable number of cases where humans behave badly and deny it, there is a perverseness which is frightening. Some analysts are convinced that this is caused by a deprivation of attention and love in early childhood. That suggests that this flaw in some humans is *caused*. And it further suggests that the way our society is treating all too many of its children nowadays is bound to bring about a large increase in later perverseness. "You can't change human nature," the old saying goes, but we're giving it a good try, for the worse.

Thinking like that always draws me up short. How did I get to be so lucky? I am loved. The perverseness in me is held in check by loving connections and gratitude. It amounts to something like the old Christian notion of grace. My life is a gift. The connections I have with other people are clues for me that life itself is not meaningless, not random.

27. SUCCESS AND PROSPERITY

Sociologists, like Troeltsch and Weber, have enjoyed linking Calvinism with the rise of capitalism. The theology taught that worldly wealth, like everything else, came from God, and that a great deal of worldly wealth was a sure sign of God's grace and favor. However, Calvinists were no good at enjoying themselves, so the wealth piled up, and there was little to do with it except plow it back into the business, which made the business prosper even more. Paintings of Flemish and Dutch capitalists of the 1600s show that they prospered, and that they didn't derive much pleasure from it beyond the smug assurance that they were God's chosen people.

I did not grow up in that sort of wealthy snobbery, thank goodness. My mother kept clear at all times my proletariat roots. They were Scottish lowland coal miners—"worrrrkin' men," and she was proud of them. My father came from German Pietist peasant stock. I still carry in my hip pocket, at all times, a red bandanna as my handkerchief. It's my peasant-proletariat flag.

When I left my little hometown and discovered the role Presbyterians play in the rest of the country—upper middle and plain old upper upper class owners of things, "owners of the means of production"—I felt like a farmer just come to the city, or a coal miner just up from underground. I was not at home.

In seminary, we students had fierce arguments about our "careers." I joined those strange ones who were saying, "It's not our task to be successful. It's our place to be faithful." Dietrich Bonhoeffer's writings inspired us more than Calvin or his contemporary professorial successors.

Who decides what success is, anyway? Was John Foster Dulles, world-renowned Presbyterian layman at that time, a success? Was Billy Graham, no Presbyterian but a well-known clergyman at that time, a success? Was the pastor of the local fat-cat Presbyterian church best described by an acerbic old elder as "oleaginous," a success? Was the pastor of the church dominated by military officers and atomic weapons engineers, who could imagine Jesus throwing bombs on little children, a success? He took in more than five times the salary I did.

And in what sense was I faithful? I merely quit, and got out. And in the end I had to redefine what I had faith in, or wanted to have faith in.

Since then, I have decided that success is another of those idols, and that I must be careful not to waste much of my energy and attention and life pursuing her. I have called her "that Bitch-Goddess," and have observed how she can tease and disappoint and waste one's time. Sure, I'd like to have a novel of mine converted into a successful movie. Sure, I'd like to have hundreds of thousands of people find and buy and read and approve of my novels and short stories. Sure, I'd like to be thought of as someone who contributed something worthwhile to the literature of the world.

I have kept fame and fortune at bay so far. A literary agent put one of the reasons succinctly, "You break all the rules of writing." Well, I don't do any such thing. My sentences parse, my plots conclude—but I do break all, or at least some, of the rules of best-seller writing, which is what the agent meant. I let what I write have its own essence, its own being. I don't try to force it into someone else's set of rules. It takes on a kind of life of its own, and my task is to capture it on paper and let it be what it is.

An instance comes to mind. After the publication of *A World For the Meek*, someone asked me, "Why'd you put *that* in?" It was a scene that has offended some and caused some librarians to refuse to shelve the novel. At first I was perplexed by the question. I didn't "put it in." It was in, before I had any say at all. My decision was, "Should I leave this in?" And since it was an integral part of the rest of it, I decided it should stay with little difficulty. That may have helped to prevent "success," as the world defines it. But I feel I had to be faithful to what I was writing, that is, to the integrity of the novel.

Even as I question the lure of success, I realize that I, like everyone else, need some kind of approval—not of the media and the establishment, nor the masses, but of somebody. I have been very fortunate to have that kind of approval. There is my wife, who

Prophet With No God

helps keep me faithful to—whatever it is—"the work," we call it sometimes. There are a few friends who "get it," who see what I am trying to do with the writing. Every once in a while an unsolicited and unexpected confirmation and acknowledgement of the worth of the results of all the effort comes through.

I am very grateful for those signals, almost abjectly so. The rest of life reminds me of that annoying Biblical story, in which Jesus tells his disciples what to expect in the way of praise or thanks: "So you, when you have done all that is commanded you, say, 'We are unprofitable servants; we have only done what was our duty.'"

"Unworthy slaves" would be a better translation of the key phrase. "Don't expect thanks," it plainly means. Don't hope for approval. Don't hope for "results" from all your effort. Just do it, and shut up about it. Results are not your affair.

"It only happens when you aren't looking." That's a proverb I made up long ago, after noticing when good things come along. It's still true. I sometimes practice the Zen method of marketing, which the world of modern business is so quick to mock. Money spent on advertising is wasted. Attempts to create publicity are demeaning. So, do the work. Write it. Create it. Let the world find it. Let the world beat its path to the door, if it will, but don't expect much. It's the same old story: "It's not up to you to be successful, but rather faithful."

In two major instances in my life, I discovered that a good resounding failure was good for the soul. The first was the collapse of support in the ecclesiastical institution. It forced me to finish the task of rethinking what I believed and what I was going to do with what was left of my life. That thinking has given me more of a sense of actually having a life, rather than being a piece of wreckage on the edge of things.

The other failure was the divorce. Whatever else divorce is, it is also a failure. Something you wanted to work, something you put yourself into, didn't pan out. I was fortunate that I didn't need to wallow long in guilt and regret, but was able to concentrate on getting it right the second time. Without the previous failure, the second marriage would not be as solid and as good as it is.

In a dream workshop, we were asked to prepare a personal "coat of arms." It included things like, Who has influenced me most? Where do I feel most at home? What adjectives describe me? The last section was "What is your greatest success in life?" I wrote, "This second marriage." When we went around the room sharing what we had written, my wife replied to that same question, "This marriage." I was greatly touched—she was on the other side of the room and had not seen what I had written. It is a kind of success.

"Prosperity," on the other hand, is something else. It has become a term that many New Age types bandy about. As they use it, it includes good health, fulfilling relationships and money, but their view of it makes me pensive. They claim to have some esoteric clue to guaranteeing these things and imply that if you don't have them it's some kind of fault of yours.

I have good health, better in my forties, fifties and sixties than before. No more backaches, no more colds. I attribute it to the lack of stress in the second marriage, mostly. Health and good relationships.

So, what about money? I have done a great deal of hard work, all my life, and have had precious little money to show for it. Truck farm labor as a boy and young man, at lower than minimum wage. But I learned gardening! College jobs, often several at a time, just to stay in school. Student pastor for four years, at one-half minimum salary, which was *low*. Missionary pastor for eight years, at minimum salary. School teacher for ten years, before salaries began to rise into the range of respectability. Scrounger for ten years, in which "living by faith" became a reality and not a theological catch phrase, even as my faith was being reconstructed from the ground up. Writer, publisher, waiting for the moon shot to bring in compensation for all the effort. Caner of chairs, for cash

Prophet With No God

flow, but not at an hourly wage much above minimum—this aspect of my work makes me feel kin to craftsmen and even most artists, who cannot charge what the hours of work, to say nothing of the know-how, are really worth.

I have become convinced that everyone needs some kind of "body work," some kind of bodily discipline. Christianity does not have it anywhere in the tradition, unless you count that abuse and neglect of the body that is asceticism. I'm no ascetic. I like eating good-tasting food. I like sex. I like music. I like art and beauty. Ascetics seem arrogant, to me.

We need some daily exercise, which I call body work, so we have gone to the orient to borrow. We tried yoga, but had stumbled on a bad teacher and injured ourselves. Then we found Tai Ch'ih. We do an Americanized version of it, Tai Ch'ih Chih, in contrast to the more commonly known Tai Ch'ih Chuan, and have done it every day for seventeen years. We believe it accounts for our good health and remarkable energy level.

I am convinced that everyone needs some kind of hand work, also. Women have an advantage here. Activities like knitting, crochet and quilting are still thought of as "women's work." They are the sort of hand work that has a healing effect on those who do them, and provide that necessary sense of accomplishment. "I did that. I brought that into being."

Gardening provides that for me, for about half the year. My emphasis has shifted from vegetables to flowers over the years. The process becomes less utilitarian and more healing.

The caning is my hand work. I get more approval from the world for my caning than for the writing and publishing. I always have some to do. When I didn't, in the past, I turned to basketry, and will again, if I ever catch up to all the chairs that keep coming my way that need caning.

So I am prospering. Even the caning, which my mind and my body thoroughly enjoy doing, is part of the prosperity. Work to do and whatever it takes to do it—isn't that prosperity?

And this writing obsession, which verges on "scriptomania"? Sometimes I think I fear worldly success in that area, since it seems to lead to untruth, to insincerity, to pretence, to compromise. I fear all that, and thus I fend off what the world calls success. It's a puzzle I fret about much less now than I used to, for which I am thankful. I'll yet learn the Zen method of marketing, and be content.

PART III

◆

BIG QUESTIONS REMAIN

28. MEMORY

For some reason, the human faculty of memory has become a major theme in my life. I have written a novel entitled *Nostalgia: A Novel of Memory*. It began as my attempt to understand my relationship as a middle-aged man to each of my parents, but it became a study of memory itself, what it is and how it works.

It seems to me that it is important to remember. I am always put off by the command or suggestion to forget. "Forget that." "You'll just have to forget that." I will not, and do not want to, forget "that," or anything else.

When I quit teaching school "to write," my first effort was to record every prepubescent memory I could dredge up. I became a teenager two weeks before Hiroshima Day, so I took the end of the war as the cut-off date. Everything before that I tried to remember and write down. The farthest back I could go was that dream/Voice, "Harry! Harry!"

I wrote on loose sheets and shifted them and added and rearranged. It took almost two years. Family, neighbors, toys, the house, the town, the creek, learning to swim, the cousins from out of town, vacations at the ocean beach, peers, girls, school, sex, the war, work on the farm, the bicycle, church—as I wrote one memory and everything connected to it that came into my mind, I would think of other things. I'd remember more, and write myself little notes on the side on scrap paper: "the fire," "the pill," "Uncle

Will and the Aurora Borealis." I worked on one little note at a time, trying to get it down, to clarify the memory, and while I was doing that, I'd be adding three or four new notes to my pile. I was getting behind. All that became four hundred typed pages. I called it a novel, but it wasn't. Some of the material is now in *Nostalgia*.

Nostalgia itself began as a play, *Grandpap and Moses*. Grandpap was my father, who really did want to be called that by his grandchildren. Moses was a mixture of me as a little kid, me as what I should have said and done, and an imaginary mythological Christ-figure.

Grandpap won't talk about, or think about, dying, even though it's one of the few things he has left to do. Moses knows all about it—he can remember being born, and hasn't been stupefied by schools.

Grandpap claims to believe in the resurrection, because it's part of what Christians are expected to believe. Moses makes gross fun of the idea and refers to cycles, the roundness, and reincarnation. "The Whole Thing is all right," he assures Grandpap, even though individual precious little egos may not be.

It was liberating for me to write it and see it on the stage. One reviewer compared it to *The Death of Ivan Ilyitch*, by Tolstoy. The other missed the first act and misunderstood the rest and spent her space referring to my once having been a clergyman. That's art and the media!

The play company wanted a better title. One came in an exchange with my wife. We were watching television, someone was singing an old love song. I commented aloud in the middle of it that if she really meant what the words said—"we're through, Buddy, and it's too late to change it!"—she wouldn't be singing at him so seductively. Adela resented the interruption of the song itself. "Just listen. Don't come with all your explanations."

"Sure. But an explanation does exist, if anyone wants one."

"Well, then," she barked, turning away from the television

image, "Explain this moment!"

I looked around—the fire in the fireplace, the last of a marvelous dinner, our cozy little nest, herself!—I couldn't. *Explain This Moment* became the title of the play. "It changes while I think about it," Moses says to his mother, when she turns on him for demanding explanations for everything.

During rehearsal it became clear that this play was my message to my father, which I couldn't deliver because he wouldn't let me speak as an adult. The message was, in a word, "I love you, but I must get on with my own life."

After the play closed, I asked myself, "What do you have to say to your mother, Harry?" I wrote another play, *When You Wish*. Every good play can be summarized as a question. In *Explain This Moment* the question was, "Can Grandpap change in time to die with dignity and grace?" In *When You Wish* the question was, "Can Sally change in time to do some living?" My father was ten years older than my mother and not at all well, so the plays seemed to fit into reality.

In each play I widowed the protagonist, unaware at the time that that might mean something profound. I think all I was doing was trying to focus on each one as an individual and not half of a couple.

Both plays are fantasy, not at all what really happened. Meanwhile I thought of a third one—why not write a trilogy?—and the third one would be, "What would really happen if I went back there after being away ten years?"

Nostalgia became too big to confine to a stage. Instead it became a rather ambitious four-layer psychological novel. One layer is the imagined contemporary visit of a middle-aged man to his aging parents whom he hasn't seen in ten years. He has these play scripts in his luggage, but isn't sure he should mention them, much less show them. The second and third layers are the plays—chunks of one or the other break out on the page of the novel unannounced. The fourth layer, in vivid technicolor, as I envision the movie, consists of some of those early childhood memories.

The irony is that the protagonist, so dedicated to memory, to remembering it without repression and error and rationalization and omission, discovers in his exploration with each parent and a sister and a grown childhood chum that memory is undependable. Some of the memories are wrong, in one head or another. Ego is the main culprit, but there are also things like creeping decrepitude and the pace of change out there in the world.

I'm convinced that it is still better to remember—to make the effort. History as a social science has become suspect—we can see the writers of it changing it, lying about it. But my own private history is in there inside me somewhere, and I think it is worth the trouble to try to remember it as honestly and completely as I can. Self-deception is an ever lurking danger and needs to be resisted. Maybe my view of all this is a holdover from Christianity or, more likely, from the Hebrew prophets. They thought that the great crime of the people was, "You forget to remember!"

The process is very tricky. Holocaust museums are fine, especially in the face of Neo-Nazis who now claim that the Holocaust never happened. But the message can be blunted and deflected a dozen ways. The Israelis say, "Never again!" and we think they surely must mean, "This kind of thing must never be allowed to happen again!" But it has happened again, and is happening again even as I write this. And some who say, "Never again!" don't mean what we think of first. They mean, "It must never again happen to us!" The clue is that some of them are now doing it to others.

Memory, along with everything else, can be corrupted by money and power. But that's no excuse to wallow in forgetting. Persons who think that the past is bunk, or boring, lack an awareness that could be helpful in comprehending the future.

Big Questions Remain 171

Reviewing one's own personal history can be especially liberating, or at least it has been for me.

This leads me to consider what I believe about what is called "therapy." Sometimes therapy appears to be setting up a nearly permanent relationship of dependence. I know people who have been in therapy for twenty years. It makes a nice income for therapists, but seems to be of questionable value to the client. I almost wrote "victim."

A friend of mine tells me that her mother cost her $200,000.

That's how much she has spent on therapy, which she needed because of what her mother did to her. But she's through with therapy now. She has declared her independence. She has used the process to remember, to find out, and is now launched in her own life. It comes to that finally: So they did all that to you. So you let them. So now what are you going to do with the rest of your life? Well, go and do it.

Memory has to do with history. Christianity is rooted in history, it says of itself. It worships "The God of history"—as if "God" was inventing history as it unrolls. I have come to believe that history is what the winners say happened, told in a way that justifies all the criminal action. Wars and elections—if there was a God inventing all that and revealing himself through it, he should be ashamed of himself.

Christianity is obsessed with the past—history, tribal and ethnic loyalty, the Jews, the saints, the missionaries. And Christianity puts the individual devotee in the past all too much—the crucifixion of Jesus, and the sins of the individual's childhood.

Then Christianity leaps to the future—the end of the world, or to the first five minutes after the individual dies, and tries to focus attention on that, on what is happening or will be happening to the ego then. Judgement, punishment, reward, all that in the future. Many serious Christians are mortgaging this life for the sake of something in the future, all the way beyond the boundary of this life.

It took me a while to find oriental philosophy. Aldous Huxley's novels were eye-opening, especially *Island*. "Here and now, boys." The mynah birds chanted essential truth! "Pay attention! Here and now, boys." Not by and by.

The *Tao Te Ching* was a floodlight of new insight for me, like the old prophets. The droll humor, especially aimed at the wounded ego, was healing. I found Zen very calming and helpful. The Whole Thing is all right.

"Explain This Moment" as a title, or just as a phrase to drop on myself or anyone else around, became very helpful. Here and now, boys. Pay attention. Explanations are of secondary value, compared to being right here now. And death, which the play is really all about, is part of the process. It doesn't have to discolor everything that precedes it, and does not need to be feared when its time comes.

29. HEALTH CARE

The exercise of preparing this enquiry into what I believe, with this lengthened perspective that comes from being in my seventh decade, serves to highlight for me the ironies of life.

All the current flap about our nation's failed health care system is amusing, as long as the observer isn't sick or injured or part of the left-out one-third of the population. Health care is another of those things Americans are willing to pay for and not get. I used to say the same thing about education to my private school students. It was mostly lost on them, since so many of them were deliberately not getting it in order to punish their unaware parents, who were paying for it.

Health care seems a little more urgent than education. You pay the insurance company for it, but when you need it, it's not there.

In my personal experience, outpatient surgery, with no meal and no bed, cost one thousand dollars an hour, and the insurance company paid only half of it.

My father sold life insurance for a living when I was a child, and as I grew up I became convinced that he didn't really believe in it. It's a form of gambling, and the bet is about mortality and the statistics about that, which are called "actuarial tables." I have since become convinced that life insurance is, as Mennonites and others say, "contrary to Christian faith." Do you trust your Heavenly Father to take care of you, as Jesus exhorts, or don't you? I think this troubled my father. He never made any money selling it, even though other agents did. He thought of it essentially as burial insurance. "The undertaker will get most of it," I often heard him say.

The insurance company gambles that you'll live a long time, and takes money from you every month, beginning immediately. You're gambling that you'll die young, and win the bet. You win by dying. The insurance company gets you to enter this strange wager by playing on your love of family and sense of responsibility to them. They win—the family, that is—by your dying. And so help me, there is a strange lack of faith in the Cosmos in all this.

And now this kind of gambling fever has infected, or rather taken over, the health care business. The company gambles that you won't get sick. You gamble that you will get sick or injured. You win by getting very sick or very badly injured very young. This hypochondriac population of ours, heavily into eating and smoking and drinking and not exercising, does indeed get sick a lot. So the companies, in danger of losing this gamble, and in the name of deregulation and amid much false preaching about the evils and dangers of socialism, figures out how to both increase the premiums you pay *and* refuse to pay for what you thought was covered. You can't read, let alone understand, the fine print, but it is all in favor of the company and designed to cheat you and make the gamble unfair. Rigged, it is.

Health Management Organizations are no better, really. I belong to one of these. I throw the premium away every month, thinking to myself, "It's anti-DWI insurance." We have the worst rate of automobile accidents caused by persons driving while intoxicated of any state in the nation. I don't want to wake up from a crash at an intersection in which a drunk ran the red light and learn that I owe some hospital and some staff of surgeons $750,000. I want to be able at least to suggest that the HMO pay some of it.

I find I can't get at the HMO doctors. It takes more than two weeks to get an appointment. I have never had a bleeding emergency, and I don't want one. HMOs are as much of a gamble as insurance companies. They gamble that you'll pay the premium and not get sick. You gamble that you'll get sick or be injured and the HMO will have to take care of you. They gamble that they can put you off and keep costs low, and still come out ahead.

I don't believe in the military analogy used by modern medicine, anyway—that disease is an invasion that must be attacked, defended against and defeated by calling in foreign mercenary troops (drugs!), or scorched earth (surgery!). My wife and I keep ourselves well by eating well, sleeping well, working hard, airing our negative emotions when they arise. I yell in traffic, and she doesn't like that and yells at me, and it's all well-ventilated that way. We don't bottle up our feelings. Everyone knows what we think, about this, or about that. And we stay well, by staying away from the medical establishment.

Well, I'm not the first person to figure out the health care situation. They have it figured out very well in Canada and Cuba. The only reason I spend this much time on it here in this enquiry is that I myself very nearly became a doctor. I went to Lafayette College in 1949 with full intent of creating an academic record that would get me into medical school. I did just that—Phi Beta Kappa in my junior year, and *summa cum laude* at graduation, and an acceptance at the University of Pennsylvania School of Medicine. But I did not want to go.

The point is, I have never regretted the decision not to become a doctor. The wealth that was passed up has never been a temptation. Missionary doctors were going out of style, even then. There are a few poor rural missionary-type doctors left, and maybe I could have been one of them, but I'm convinced that it was better for me this way.

The doctors have become the new priests. The general population of this culture is not allowed to feel well, to feel good, to eat this or drink that, or do anything at all, without first consulting the doctor. My wife and I don't even have a doctor. Large numbers of people believe everything the doctor says, and even everything the actor dressed like a doctor on TV commercial messages says. They consult this new priesthood as if it were some kind of oracle.

The doctor has replaced the priest as the key person to deal with individual mortality. Some are not very good at it. They think of Death as the great adversary, and when his winning move is finally inexorable, they feel defeated. Meanwhile they have invented marvelous devices and procedures to delay that final move. The procedures ultimately don't work, of course. You die anyway.

I'm glad I'm not involved in that process, as doctor or pastor. I find myself entirely in sympathy with Dr. Kavorkian, who is confronting the matter head-on and admittedly helping people end their lives, when modern medical technology has made what's left of life totally miserable. I'm told that many doctors are doing the same thing, while deploring Kavorkian's lust for publicity. I'm glad that so many are that sensitive, that aware of the human condition and their own limitations as life preservers, but I salute him also for his willingness to create a fuss in hopes of getting laws changed.

How do we change the American lust to live forever? It's not merely human. Many cultures have not had it. Elderly and infirm

Eskimos used to go out onto the ice to die and relieve the group of a burden. Read *Top of The World*. The elderly in primitive Japan knew that the time would come when they would have to separate from the group and die, for the good of the group. See the film *Ballad of Narayama*. In contemporary Netherlands they have changed the role of the medical doctor in the dying process.

And now, see what I am doing? Acting in my role as mythologist, while rejoicing that I am not a doctor. Another book of mine, *Myth and Mortality*, goes into this at length. It took many years to write, beginning when my parents died. That story will have to be part of this enquiry.

30. MORTALITY

I didn't see my parents for ten years because of the way they treated my second wife. She thought it was simply racism, since she's a chicana, and we do communicate a lot in Spanish. I think some of it was a sense of scandal about divorce and remarriage.

During that ten-year period I dreamed of my hometown a great deal. It fascinated the dream groups that I was facilitating. One group was especially helpful to me. "You must give up the neurotic hope that they'll ever treat you like an adult and allow an adult relationship with you. They won't; it won't happen." The group helped me do it, give up that hope, which was neurotic—wanting what can't be, what can't be had. It was as though my parents died. I grieved with tears and heartache and all. But I grew up and got over it.

In the midst of a raging snowstorm, the same one during which an airplane fell into the Potomac River, I flew back east for the first time in ten years. The messages from my sisters were that my father was dying. I decided not to leave a residue that would require dredging later. I wanted to make this as clean as possible. When I arrived, he was not dying. The emphysema had caused an embolism, an air bubble in the brain like a stroke, but which left little or no brain damage. The subsequent medication *was* killing him, and making him very crazy at the same time, but the doctors figured that out and took him off it while I was flying.

The first greeting told the whole story. "My boy came home! Aren't you my little boy?"

"No, I'm not. I'm a man. I'm an old man!" I was months from fifty.

"Well, I didn't mean *little*."

"But that's what you keep saying."

They were delighted with the visit, and I was not. It was surface stuff, avoiding confrontation. It was duck and dodge memories, keep up appearances for the neighbors' sake—just what they wanted, but not at all what I had wanted so very much and had given up finally, so painfully. I felt distant, like a stranger in a miniaturized illusion, a movie set that looked a little at times like "home," like my memories of home, but wasn't home at all.

Two years later a member of that dream group and I went on a cross-country bus trip together to accompany each other in digging up childhood. We did my old hometown first. I felt more distant than ever. I let Ed do the arguing with my sister, who had become a militant Reaganite, obsessed with fear of what she called "Soviet domination." This was in 1984. My one insertion into the discussion was, "My God, they can't even dominate Poland," but mostly I kept silent. The fear of Soviet domination seems comical now, but I'm not in touch with my sisters, so it matters very little.

My father hated Reagan but refused to discuss it, because he wanted the appearance, the illusion, of "peace in the family." I was quite bemused by the whole thing, really, seeing it as what it was for the first time. His principles mattered less than that precious illusion. I felt like a stranger.

By the following spring, my father was very sick. He was 88

years old, and not breathing well. Seizures, little embolisms, struck every once in a while, leaving him twitching on the floor, and furious when he woke up in the hospital, feeling as if nothing was the matter. He required much care. I called my mother, who had just turned 79. "Should I come?" I asked.

"I'd rather you came for the funeral," she said. I was put off by that at first. It seemed to be her way of manipulating, her preference for appearances, her concern for what the neighbors would think, overruling any concern about real connections. But I agreed, thinking again, "I don't want to be troubled by inner unreachable guilt after this is over. I'll go along, so it'll be clean when it's done."

"How are you?" I asked. "Shouldn't he be in a home? You'll exhaust yourself."

"It's rough. But we're doing it, one day at a time." Well, I thought, that's how we're supposed to do life, so I subsided. One sister lived 140 miles away, and came most weekends. The other lived five miles away and checked in on the way to or from work every day.

Adela got a call from Sue, the nearby sister. Sue found Mom dead that morning. She was sitting on a backless stool near the telephone, with her head leaned back against the wall. It didn't even knock her to the floor.

So, the funeral I went back to was *her* funeral.

Ann, the sister a little further away, the one who loved Reagan, reacted strangely to Sue's telling me, "He killed her! He killed her!"

I asked Sue what that meant.

"You'll find out."

The sisters set up a schedule, in writing, and required that all of us—siblings, offspring, girlfriends of offspring, offspring of offspring, everyone—take turns "taking care of Grandpap."

I asked why.

"So everyone knows how Mama died. What she was trying to do. What he did to her. What killed her."

Well, it was a revelation. Before the end of my first shift, I told him, "You know, this care that you need so much of—wipe your forehead, give you a drink, move the towel—it doesn't add up to anything at all. It looks to me like what you want is someone to assure you every two minutes that you haven't died yet. You look afraid."

"Of course, I'm afraid," he said, looking very afraid.

"Why? After all you taught us about God and Jesus and forgiveness and salvation and heaven? Why are you afraid?" He gave his head one negative shake.

Without intending or deciding anything, without rehearsing my lines at all, I became the one who represented his next task to him. "You call yourself a Follower of the Way." He always loved that single reference to the early Christians in the Book of Acts. "Close your eyes. Do you see a path?" He gave that negative shake of the head. "No, I won't hush. See that road, that Way? You must make your journey up that way."

It did no good. He resisted every attempt. Once I turned away, muttering more to myself than anyone, "His mythology let him down." I began writing *Myth and Mortality* at that moment. His mythology let him down. What about mine? Is anyone else interested in this topic, that is, what we really believe about our mortality?

My muttered statement was offensive to some in the room. One fundamentalist nephew resented my calling Christianity mythology. My sisters told me so later, as we killed a bottle of tequila together. I was sorry, but speaking as a professional mythologist, I had to insist that Christianity was and is mythology. What my comment meant was, "His belief system, the one he taught us so well that it took me forty years to get out from under it, the one that claims to provide victory over Death for its adherents—all that psychological and 'spiritual' superstructure—let him down. It isn't working. He is afraid to die, and for an ardent Christian, that's a scandal."

I began to understand my mother's not wanting me to come. She did not want me to see my father's lack of faith. What I was doing, challenging him to gather up his courage and go ahead and die, would have upset her very much. Sue told me of how she had tried to warn Mom, "You must limit him."

"Yer faither's daein'!" exclaimed Mom, in her Scottish tongue.

"Well, you be careful, or he'll be the death o' you first," said Sue, who sounded more Scottish than usual, using a phrase Mom had often used when she was out of patience with us as little children.

Mom didn't want me in on such a scene. I heard it in my imagination—her telling *me*, "Yer faither's daein'!"—and my retort, "Aye, 'n' whyn't he gie on wi' it?" I could talk Scottish, too, when emotionally charged.

So, she died at her post. As I wrote all this up, beginning work on the book, I wrote of my mother, "She knew what she was doing." By dying when and as she did, I mean. She did it deliberately, fearlessly, causing no trouble to anyone else. She reached the end of her store of energy, and laid her burden down.

I gathered stories from other cultures, of how dying is accepted as part of the cycle of life, and of how individuals can muster the wherewithal from inside themselves to say goodbye and then simply put in and die.

My father was the great contrast, it seemed to me. He resisted; he demonstrated fear. Scenes from the film *Ballad of Narayama* came vividly into my mind before and after my mother's funeral: The old lady in the story smashed her teeth out deliberately at the village well in order to qualify for the trip to Narayama, the mountain on the other side of a deep ravine where the elderly and infirm were taken to die among the skeletons and the crows. She insisted that her middle-aged son carry her there and leave her. He was having difficulty, but was doing his duty. On the climb up they met a man carrying his aged father. The old man had tied himself fast to the son, and at the top would not get off the rack that held him on his son's back. The son had to force him, yanking on the rope, loosening it, untying the terrified old man, finally picking him up bodily and flinging him over the edge of the cliff, screaming, "Go! Go to Narayama!"

I didn't throw my father over, but I encouraged him to go on his own. He would not. He lost his belief in forgiveness and salvation. They were not for him, after all. He shook his head, "No." Did he see such doctrines as fundamentally immoral after all, as I do now? Or was he psychologically so wounded, by things that happened long before my time, that he couldn't let the Good News apply to himself?

He never was interested in the ideas that were doing me so much good—oriental and Native American ideas, mostly, about cycles and roundness and recurrence and reincarnation. He never paid any attention to any of that, since it wasn't Christian. He couldn't understand my interest in dreams, even though there's plenty of that in the Bible.

I was cross at him for teaching me what he didn't believe himself. I had a little of Ann's reaction—why did he need to drag Mom down, depriving her of her widowhood and a chance to live, a little?

We put him in a nursing home the afternoon of the funeral. He resisted all my admonitions, which statements absolutely scandalized the staff of the facility, that it was time for him to "be on his journey."

It did no good. I left thinking he'd live for years—stubborn, contrary, bullheaded. That was my mother's description of him many a time. But, no, I received a call ten days later. He had died in the night.

I wondered in what state of mind he died. No one knows. Did he die peacefully? Did he greet Death willingly at last? Did he jump? Or did he finally crash, after all the frantic efforts to stay alive in spite of total bodily collapse? In my heart I hope he jumped.

At my father's funeral I recalled with chagrin the funerals I conducted during an earlier part of my life. In rain, in wind, in snow, in sunshine, I accompanied people to that final resting place, mouthing phrases I could not possibly have internalized yet, because I was too young. Chanting empty ritual which may as well have been in Latin.

I recalled how it became more and more difficult as I gradually awakened. I used to marvel at what other pastors would say at funerals. What? Who are we burying here? That's not the man I knew! At least I never deliberately stated what I knew wasn't true. But I did mouth the ritual, even after I knew I no longer believed "...in the sure and certain hope of the final resurrection at the last..." I'm glad I don't conduct funerals anymore.

I wrote an account of the details of the two funerals of my parents, and what led up to them, interspersed with poetry that came pouring out at the time in quiet moments, on airplanes, at a desk, wherever.

I found that I had already been through grief, back when the neurotic hope had died. Others at my parents' funerals no doubt found me callous. I found myself impatient with the easy answers of the fundamentalists, including those in the family.

There was a considerable sense of liberation, and no guilt about that, yet nevertheless Death felt heavy. For weeks I was unaccountably exhausted. My thoughts dwelled on our mortality, on my mortality, while I wrote *Myth and Mortality* (entitled at first *Myths To Die By*, in homage to Joseph Campbell's *Myths To Live By*).

In order to write it, I read many books by Eastern and Western philosophers. I looked at our culture from a new angle and saw how confused and moribund it is. I clarified how great a disservice fundamentalism performs for those who allow themselves to be at all influenced by it. I rewrote the thing four times, reorganizing the material, making it more and more clear to myself. As I rewrote, I removed the anger at my father that came through in early drafts.

Two introductory essays deal with why the subject of mortality needs additional attention: "The Denial of Death" and "We Need a New Mythology." They contain the analysis of the cultural confusion. Old church authority is gone; the old message is no longer believed, in spite of outward protestations. And the fact of death is denied. We spend hundreds of billions on megadeath, even without an outward enemy to aim it all at, and spend almost nothing on any kind of awareness of our own personal mortality. We try to keep the teenager's illusion of invulnerability intact all the way to the brink of the abyss.

Then, after these essays, I analyze more than thirty different beliefs, or stories, or metaphors, arranged in six groups. They range all the way from infantilism ("Daddy will come fix it," "The world is my plaything"), to religion ("Only our group has the truth," "The resurrection of the body"), to philosophy ("Absorption in the One," "Reincarnation"). One thing I noticed in the process: Religion tends to enhance and preserve ego, while philosophy tries to transcend ego and get beyond it.

There is a concluding essay, "Whose Task Is This?" I can already imagine that some readers, when they get to this last part, will misunderstand it—"You're suggesting that old people just go away and die!"

I am not suggesting that. I am suggesting that people my age begin now to think seriously about all this, seriously enough that we will be able to take steps to make sure that we do not become expensive vegetables in medical warehouses or castoff, worthless, mindless, empty shells in nursing homes. I think we should be working hard to change laws concerning unwanted medical care that prolongs what can no longer be called "life" while transferring funds to the medical establishment. I think we must neutralize the political power of fundamentalists and the Roman Catholic hierarchy, who deny that we are responsible for all of our lives, including the time and manner of our death. Mostly, I want this discussed more than it now is, without the authoritarians shouting down the rest of us.

I want for myself the courage to be in charge of my life until the end of it and, if necessary, to bring the end closer even though modern medical technology might be capable of hindering that some.

There are stories, whole traditions, in which the infirm face the truth of their existence and take action while they still can. It isn't even suicide exactly. They don't need a weapon. They have learned how to live, and then they learn how to die, and then when the time comes, they just do it.

One of the yogis that I read says that the inability to fall asleep is a disease, an illness. So, likewise, he says, is the inability to die. Can we learn how to do this? Can I learn it—that's the question—so that when the time comes, before nursing home, before Alzheimer's, before utter impoverishment of my family and community, before any of that, I can hie me off to the next stage of life? Or to Blotto, if that's what awaits? I want the wherewithal to do that for myself. Can we talk about it? Can we share letters with one another about it?

A dear friend told about her mother, whose mind was failing, who was becoming an impossible burden for the husband, age ninety, and for my friend. "There should be someone who tends to this," the old lady said.

"Tends to this?"

"Not the doctor. Someone who would come and tend to this."

"This" was that slow, slow slide, that drift into vacuity and helplessness, while the body, with no mind in it to torment it further, goes on and on, and caregivers are slowly but surely drained utterly of energy and even love. The Tender, the tender Tender, would come and bring all that horror to an end, sometime nearer the beginning of that slide, before all the caregivers were drained and dead.

While I was thinking all that and writing all that and reading all the related things, people wondered if I wasn't becoming morbid, obsessed with dying. One asked, "Have you had a medical report about yourself that you're not sharing with us?" No. I'm healthier than I was in my twenties. Not as strong, to be sure, but more *alive*. I want to be alive all the while, until I'm dead. I am greatly troubled by the people I know whose lives are derailed and even threatened by the fact that someone they love, a parent usually, cannot get past that last gate, cannot die. I don't want to do that to anyone, to linger on without purpose or hope for recovery.

I came out with another insight, after paying all that attention to dying. The best preparation for dying is to pack in a lot of living. Both Adela and I are doing that. I have much I still want to do, unfinished novels especially. I find myself no longer frantic about that, but am learning to lean back and allow it, rather than think that I'm being pressed to do it. And all the while I'm aware of Death on my shoulder, watching. He is no longer an enemy. He's just part of my life. I can imagine my mother greeting him with a smile. I hope to be able to do the same, when the time comes. I'll not run from him, nor will I bar the door against him. That's a hopeless venture, anyway.

In my short play "Soliloquy With Five Interruptions," which is part of the novel *This'll Kill Ya*, an old, old man is celebrating his birthday alone. It is raining and raining outside his little adobe house. His grandson and family have gone away on a trip. Oldtimer reminisces about his life, his wives, his family, his understanding of what matters in life and what doesn't. As he tells it, we note a contrast between his practical and generous views and the narrow-minded, doctrinaire, uptight views of the absent "religious" grandson.

The first two interruptions are the neighbors, come to warn him and urge him to evacuate with them on foot—there's going to be flooding. Oldtimer declines to go.

The third and fourth interruptions are a pair of rescue workers who appear at the window in a rowboat. Again Oldtimer declines to go, but only after he has made a play for the young female worker. As they are leaving, we learn that the absent grandson is Noah, and that Oldtimer is Methuselah.

The fifth interruption is Noah's Flood. The text in Genesis does not state it, but if one does the arithmetic of the begats in all that genealogy, the figures indicate that Methuselah died in the year of the Flood. My poetic license allowed me to indicate that Methuselah died, in his 969th year, on his birthday, *in* the Flood.

Before the final interruption, Oldtimer wonders "what happens to you when you die." He tells what I would tell, if asked, so it fits into this enquiry concerning what I believe.

What happens to you when you die? Oldtimer throws in an expanded translation of one of Adela's proverbs: *El que por su gusto muere, hasta la muerte le sabe.* "If you've really enjoyed life, tasted it all, drunk deep, every drop of all the juice, then even Death itself will taste good."

31. REINCARNATION

What happens to you when you die? Many thoughtful people whom I love and respect tell me that they believe in what I call Blotto. "When you're dead, you're dead," they say. They have a remarkable earnestness about them, a desire to "make use of the time." I believe I have some of that, too. But I have trouble with Blotto as a creed. It seems so uncharacteristic of the Universe. The compost pile seems to teach that nothing is really wasted. Forms are continually altered. Last year's leaves are no longer leaves at all. But they are not Blotto.

Human bodies die and decompose and become compost, in spite of the efforts of embalmers. Is that still all there is to it? What about that other rather marvelous achievement that some, if not all, humans are capable of, namely, consciousness, awareness? A person can spend a lifetime learning, remembering, connecting things, comprehending some things, understanding some things, drawing nearer and nearer to the truth about some things, if not all things. What then? Is that consciousness, that awareness, simply thrown away when the human body hits the compost heap? I have trouble believing that the cosmos works that way. But maybe it does. Maybe I'm wanting to inject some kind of Cosmic Purpose into my own curiosity.

I admit to being a curious person, although I see many around me who are not. If we are nothing more than compost, then all this effort to learn and remember and find out and figure out seems a ridiculous waste. The lotus-eaters of myth are right, after all, if that's the case.

I am fascinated by the notion of reincarnation. In addressing it in *Myth and Mortality*, I did for reincarnation what Dr. Kunkle did decades ago for evolution—I piled up all the assorted kinds of evidence, more than a dozen kinds. No one piece of evidence is quite enough to be utterly convincing but, all piled up there together, they are quite impressive and *almost* convincing. I concluded that it was the most likely, most believable metaphor of all those I studied.

The title of my novel *Souls and Cells Remember* tells it all, for some. We have cell memory, handed down the daisy chain of gene pool connections. I do have some things within me that seem unaccountable otherwise. A Celtic melancholy, a love of water and hopeless causes—if I learned that personally from my mother, I'm amazed. She came from Scotland, but did not like the water. How did she teach the hair on the back of my neck to rise up when I hear bagpipes? No, I suspect I inherited something—I'm calling it "cell memory." On the other side, my affinity for the German language seems to have been inherited from my father's branch, not learned.

Then there's soul memory. My childhood included a strange attachment to natives of this hemisphere that could hardly have been learned in the environment I grew up in. Deep inside me, as I learned the history of the woods of Pennsylvania, I was on the Indians' side. I found net-sinkers in the creek. I imagined traveling in a birchbark canoe. I scalped the white invaders and destroyers.

In *Souls and Cells*, my character imagines that in a previous incarnation he was the last Susquehannock. It is a steamy love story, a soul-mate story, and reincarnation is what makes the plot work. The main two characters are attracted to one another because they've been connected before.

The creation of the novel began with those strange primordial memories of mine, but after pumping up the imagination needed to write the novel, I now have trouble looking back and being sure which element *is* memory and which is imagination, and what is the novel itself, which took on a life of its own. I am startled every time I reread portions of it.

What needs noting now in this enquiry is that, after all of that, I still find myself hesitating to state flatly that I really do believe in reincarnation. I want to so much. It makes sense, I think, more sense than any other theory, including Blotto. The cosmos does not throw away what is learned from experience, after all. Some of it is saved, maybe all of it, and another go-round can include it, or some of it. It's beautiful. I want to believe it. But I'm suspicious of it. It is so enticing, I want to believe it so much, but I'm afraid of deceiving myself.

Big Questions Remain

I wonder why I'm so concerned about self-deception. Probably because I've wasted, in a sense, a great deal of time and energy on self-deception already. I'm trying to be cagey. And I may be wasting another kind of time and energy, being "cool." Maybe there is still time for whole-hog passionate belief again, but it doesn't seem likely.

What I have now is a very tentative adherence to the possibility, maybe the hope, that reincarnation is a metaphor for whatever really is going on. The old language hinders here. What is "soul"? Are souls eternal? Is anything eternal, except The Whole Thing, the Process Itself? What is the difference between the ego and the soul?

I can accept the extinction of the ego in the compost pile. In fact, I really am working on that, in advance. Death loses its sting when I don't identify with ego, but with something deeper, something higher. But what is it? Self? That's the oriental word for it. The Self of the World. But there's only one of them. In what sense am I it? If I'm not the perishable ego, then what? What was it that was once a Susquehannock beside Loyalsock Creek and returned two centuries later as a sad Scottish-German boy—with Susquehannock memories? I have better questions than answers, and I've noticed that before.

I recall word studies in those Hebrew classes in seminary. "God breathed into his nostrils the breath of life, and man became a living soul." That's the old translation. "A living being" is the RSV—not much of a translation. *Nephesh chayah.* What is *nephesh*? What has *nephesh*? The ancient Hebrews were not animists, who would say that everything has *nephesh*, all animals and trees, and even rocks and mountains and clouds.

No, the Hebrews didn't think that rocks and trees and earth had *nephesh*—that's why their mythological world view, taken over by the Christians later, has been so destructive of the environment. They don't think it has *nephesh*; there's nothing in there—in a tree, or a forest, or a mountain—that can be hurt by being destroyed. It's clear to me that I'm more of an animist than a Hebrew/Christian, but we need to get back to *nephesh*.

Nephesh is something in a human being and, according to the Hebrews, also in the animals that are fit for sacrifice, like sheep and goats, but not in others, like lizards and mice. It's a something that was received directly from God, that makes it what it is, alive. "A living being" won't translate it. Mice are alive, too. "A living soul" is better, but we still have to figure out "soul."

"Your eternal soul" is a phrase used by fundamentalist preachers to terrify the non-thoughtful with threats of eternal conscious torment. My mother used a similar phrase, with a grim twist. When we had upset her, and she was into her reactive rant—which is marvelous to remember but was terrifying to experience while little—she'd shriek, "You make me damn my eternal soul!" She had an eternal soul, and she was putting it in jeopardy, and it was all our fault! Well, from this perspective fifty years later, I can flatly state that I don't believe any of that. I don't believe in eternal conscious torment of eternal souls in hell. I quit doing that, and said so, while I was still a clergyman. Christians objected to my view even then, saying that if there wasn't any hell, heaven would be no fun. That's how mean they were, meaner than any self-respecting God would ever be.

I still don't know about eternal souls. Souls are what are reincarnated, according to that metaphor. Christian theology, which rejects reincarnation, is irrational at this point. "Eternal" means "not limited by time," "outside of time." Most popular usage means "everlasting," which is the old translation and not exactly the same thing. But everlasting goes in two directions. Looking forward into an everlasting future, one can try to imagine a future that never ends, that goes on and on, forever. The mean-hearted want to add conscious torment to *that*.

But what about looking backward? "Everlasting" would mean

Big Questions Remain

looking backward, back and back, farther and farther, on and on, back and back, with no end, that is, no beginning. Hindus do it. Then the two everlasting directions meet, way out there, and we get circles, huge circles, cycles, very large and very long cycles. Hindus can do it, but Hebrews/Christians cannot. They plunk down a thing they call "creation," and stop the process, when looking backward. It is not everlasting, not eternal. It is only half-eternal. Now, that's illogical. Either something is eternal, or it isn't.

"God" is supposedly making eternal souls, either at creation or at conception. People who believe in creation don't believe in eternal souls at all, but half-eternal ones. You can tell I'm not believing it, not any of it, not even the notion that there is an Entity/Creator "God" at all. But I still have to figure out what I am, and what you are.

I am a temporary form. My body is a vehicle, quite marvelous. It does not need permission from the AMA to be healthy, happy and useful. My body already at age 62 is not as strong as it used to be. It tires sooner than it used to, and is incapable of the long hours of hard physical labor it put in formerly. I find it stiffening strangely when I keep it in the same position for long periods, even doing almost nothing, such as sitting in a chair watching a movie, or sitting at this desk writing. I sense that some day, perhaps not exactly soon, but some day imaginable, this body will give out and no longer be what we call alive. I hope the mind doesn't give out sooner; I regard that as one of the bitterest tragedies, and it's becoming more and more common today.

What do I believe that I am? I am a body which will not live forever. I wouldn't want it to. I have much to do, and feel a little pressured by the knowledge that if I intend to do it, I'd better get at it, because I don't have forever.

I am not my body, not exactly, not entirely and merely. What is there more than the body? The brain is part of the body. When that organ fails, and the rest of the body goes on freewheeling—that's the tragedy mentioned above. But I am not my brain, either. Something in the chest, the emotional center, the heart chakra—Well, what do I *know*? Better start with the facts.

The brain doesn't survive death; it can die early, in fact. The heart chakra—bah! It's too much. And all the authoritative statements that use the word "soul" are suspect, because I don't trust the sources. Especially the Christians. But even the Tibetans and the Egyptians, who could write Books of the Dead—how did they *know*? Why am I left unconvinced after reading that stuff?

And yet I can't drop it and become a mechanist. There is more to it than that, but I don't understand it yet, and probably don't have time to figure it out before the experience becomes immediate and my own. One day I'll find out for myself.

If something doesn't survive, some wisdom, some mellow insight, some advantage of perspective, then the Cosmos is wasteful and needlessly cruel. I don't believe it is. What a fragile indefinite unconvincing sort of belief that is! The fundies will laugh.

I have wrestled with this topic for a long time. I have dear friends who take reincarnation as a fact quite for granted and seem even a little glib about it. I met a woman recently who does believe in it, and the way our relationship works, without preliminaries, without having to gather data about each other over decades, seems to indicate that we've been connected before. She's quite convinced of it. "Where've you been for a thousand years? You said you were going out for a cuppa coffee!"

I do not believe the cosmos wastes anything. It doesn't always value things, especially our precious egos, and the precious works of our hands, quite the way we do, but nothing goes to waste. So, when I look at my elderly friends, with all that awareness and all that experience and all that knowledge, I wonder what the cosmos is going to do with it as the physical vehicle begins to wear out. Reincarnation is a concept that allows for some kind of recycling of what is learned. I do wish to believe in that—that all our puzzlement is not a cosmic joke, that it is better to know than to not know, that finding out is one of the great liberating experiences of existence and is worth the trouble, somehow.

Another dear friend, who also takes reincarnation quite for granted, says that life on our planet is a school, and we're here to learn things, and you can't flunk out or drop out, and all of us are learning things, and we will move up to more and more difficult lessons, and none of the learning is wasted. The cosmos is what is doing the learning.

I contemplate the size and age of the cosmos and wonder how my dinky little lessons could amount to anything. But it is true that we are all learning, each at his or her own pace. And, thank goodness, I am learning—it is the most exciting thing I do. So can I believe, then, that the Cosmos is learning, through me? And that each little life-lesson is part of that larger thing that's going on? It takes a little doing to make the leap from the mechanistic cosmos to something—*more*. But yes, I can and do believe that.

32. OPENNESS

The circumstances and experiences of my life have made me a loner. The beloved community of the church will never be able to overcome my mistrust of the institution and its doctrines. Also, I repudiate the irrational authority of government and its agencies at all levels. It seems to me that schools and teachers need to be outgrown. I do my learning and teaching on my own now. There is no group of fellow writers sustaining me in this work—I find this to be a remarkably lonely enterprise. My companions, the prophets, have been dead for millennia.

A loneliness lurks nearby more or less all the time. I have a remarkable wife, and a few close friends, but mine is essentially a loner's life. I must deal continually with my tendency to lapse into the Elijah Complex. Elijah the prophet was feeling sorry for himself; hiding from wicked Queen Jezebel, who had already killed the Lord's prophets with the sword, he said, "And I, even I only, am left, and they seek my life also to take it away." He was exaggerating, he was in error, he was wallowing in self-pity, he needed to be jolted out of it. I need it, too, from time to time. As Thoreau stated so starkly, many of my fellow humans live lives of quiet desperation. I do not, but that's because of the web of support I have.

Humans are social animals. We are formed by our connections to other people. Parents, siblings, neighbors, peers; by oneself a human being isn't anybody. When someone yells at those around him, "Leave me alone!" it's a clue to the quantity of desperation that person is feeling. Some of my fictional characters do yell that, but I do not. I admit to being a little sensitive about this, however. If I receive the slightest inkling of a hint that my presence is not wanted, I'm gone and it will be hard to get me back. I do not impose myself on anyone.

A Bible verse may be contributing to the loneliness. "Am I my brother's keeper?" Cain asked, when questioned about the whereabouts of his brother Abel. It's the wrong question, but then Cain may have been befuddled by the same emotions that made him a murderer. Nobody wants a keeper. I don't want to be anyone's keeper, either. What we all need so desperately is some sharing, some contact, some connection. We need some sense of journeying together. Tragedy occurs when injuries and betrayals cause us to close up and refuse to let others near.

Life is a flow. It flows in and it flows out. When we are closed, the flow stagnates and goes bad. I am glad for the openness that I learned, learned almost in spite of everything that happened to me. I regard it as a miracle.

I dedicated *Souls and Cells Remember* to Aphrodite. I have come to see that Desire is It, The Whole Thing, the Cosmos, whatever we're going to call it. Desire is wanting something to change. I am convinced that Desire will not be permanently thwarted by externally imposed rules nor by internalized parental prohibitions. Desire, Aphrodite, will have her way, or all hell will break loose.

I was saved by the glands once, early on—saved from narrow-minded, self-righteous, smug meanness. I was lucky. It wasn't uncaring macho sex. It was caring, gentle, bumbling, fumbling, confused, loving sex. I would be an ungrateful idiot to pretend that it didn't do me much good.

We were married, as children almost, but it was the right thing for us to do, then. Far better than sacrificing happiness and intimacy on some imaginary altar of "service to God," in an attempt to be "more pious than God." Who made us the way we are? Who invented sex? If it wasn't God, then what kind of a "God" is he claiming to be?

Decades later, having grown up, we discovered that we were more different than we realized, that we wanted and valued different things, that we were unhappy and would have become more unhappy if we remained entangled. So we separated.

I was saved again. This time it was the fellow quester I had known and shared with for more than ten years. We knew each other. After ten years of talking and thinking and questioning and growing, with no physical sexual element in the relationship, Aphrodite reared her gorgeous head, and she was irresistible. "There you are!" It was as if scales fell from my eyes. It was a conversion experience.

We married and built a solid relationship. Each one has room to be who he or she is. "You let me be who I am," one says.

"I love you, as you are, as who you are," the other replies. It's a little silly sounding, and it is awesome.

"You're not trying to change me."

"I'd be an idiot to try to change you."

There is room to grow, and there is so much talking, talking in both languages, and sharing of what we're thinking and learning, that we're not afraid of one growing away from the other. We stay in touch. We touch, a lot. I find it is all the group I need. Here I am supported, here I am affirmed, here I am thanked, for being what I am and doing what I do.

And it has left me open, still open. I have friends of the opposite sex, as the phrase goes, and it is natural. I'm not looking for anything. But I have hugs to give, and smiles, and time to listen. I've been lucky, to put it mildly, and openness has become one of the main things I believe in.

I have felt a solidarity with the have-nots of the world, those who do most of the world's work for little or no pay. The owners of the means of production do less work than those who pick the fruit and vegetables, who mine the coal, who assemble the appliances, who sew the clothes. Both my wife and I are hard workers, and have been all our lives. We like work, love to work, love to have work in front of us needing to be done. My political views reflect my awareness of our peasant-proletariat backgrounds, but also our eagerness to affirm the value of work itself and of those who do it. Now we own our own businesses, but we have never really left the working class. It is strange.

I have never been a good employer. Adela has the same problem. It is hard for her to hire needed help because of some notion that the employer is claiming to be better than, or superior to, the employee. We end up doing it ourselves for the most part, and keeping our businesses of a size that we don't need employees. Maybe this has more to do with our commitment to equality than any notion of openness, but maybe not. We can be open, because we have walked in those other moccasins.

This is the place to discuss "family values." The phrase is suspect because of who is preaching it the loudest. Jimmy Swaggart, for example. I find that "family values" is a phrase, and sort of ideal, which is part of a dying racket. Churches use the idea of family to maintain their hold on people, and to thwart the thinking process and the tendency toward liberation. Parents who don't believe a word of the doctrine take or send their children to Sunday School, where they are subjected to that psychological abuse—the teaching that they are wicked sinners—all in the name of family solidarity. It would be better if loving parents defended their children from such treatment.

In the name of "the family," persons, especially wives, are kept in situations of suffering and even danger. Divorce is regarded as sin and failure. Single parents are regarded as second-raters and somehow at fault, no matter what the underlying reasons for the situation. Pairs of parents of the same sex are frowned upon, or worse. All in the name of "family values."

The family I grew up in, which was not a scene of physical violence and abuse, was nevertheless abusive. My father used the word "love" as a weapon. He scared the pie out of his very young children with the Bible story in which Jesus repeatedly asked Peter if he loved him. For my father the evidence of love was obedience. It got to the point where, when he said "love," we knew to become wary. "Oh-oh. What does he want now?"

Grown siblings picked it up. Family unity transcends honesty, truth, values—but I find I cannot keep it up. I am not now in direct touch with my sisters. There is too much misunderstanding, too much hopelessly complicated explanation required continually. It is not worth the trouble. The superficial way of relating, which seemed to satisfy my parents toward the end, in the name of the appearance of solidarity, is not for me.

So I find the kind of brotherly connections I need and want, the unconditional positive regard that is not obligated by family connections, outside the gene pool. There are only a few of them, but they are very precious.

I found this in *The Notebooks of Malte Laurids Brigge*, by Rainer Maria Rilke, and I can't put it better:

"The Prodigal Son left home because he didn't want them to love, couldn't take their love, wouldn't let their love overwhelm him and annihilate him. He went back because he couldn't be himself without his childhood, after all, and they still misunderstood his assumption that love was now out of the question—and they loved on and on, but he was unscathed, having become himself meanwhile."

As for my offspring, I enjoy them and share with them in a very satisfying way. I have been careful not to do to them what was done to me. Their lives are not the fulfillment of mine. There is no attempt at substitution, at vicarious achievement through them. I will not control them, or attempt to in any way. More irony— sometimes I fear that the result of that caution may be a question in their minds as to whether I care much. We have talked about it, and I think they know that I do, but I err on the side of non-interference.

Openness to people is sometimes compromised by an awareness of the danger of control or interference. Not everyone wants to be all that open, at all times. And in my own case, I find that openness to new ideas and change, which is an important part of being open, is compromised by a jaundiced view of "progress," which is getting worse lately. New roads, new freeways, new housing developments, new bridges—these are not always progress. Finer and finer profit-making schemes in planned and deliberate obsolescence is not progress.

New side effects from new medicines, new hormones in the milk, new genetic alterations in plants like tomatoes—this is not always progress. New sitcoms complete with laugh track that laughs when nothing funny is going on, new shoot-em-ups that glorify new violence in new ways, new spy stories that keep new and old international tensions at fever pitch—I'm sorry, but that's not progress. New atomic bombs, new delivery systems, new chemical warfare substances, new man-made biological warfare agents—I'm not open to that stuff.

I remember getting into trouble, or at least into an argument, over my announced policy at a faculty preparation meeting for a summer camp I was to direct for the Presbyterian Synod of New Mexico in the mid-1960s. "No illegal questions," was the policy, meaning that there would be no such thing as an illegal question from the youngsters who attended this church camp. The kids could ask us adults any question that was on their minds.

"Oh, my! What if they ask about sex?"

"You can't handle questions about sex?" I replied.

"Well, but it has nothing to do with the church curriculum, does it?"

"If the kids have questions, about sex or about anything else, I want them to trust us enough to ask them."

"Shouldn't their parents be handling that?"

"Maybe they should, but it's safe to bet that they don't in every case. There shall be no illegal questions." The policy was related to my insistence on open enquiry and my dislike of secrecy. "There is nothing secret that shall not be made known." There shall be no closed topics, including the Secretary of State's mishandling of U.S. foreign policy in Southeast Asia.

Since then I have become a minor local celebrity in my opposition to censorship. My story *This'll Kill Ya: The Last Word on Censorship* was done as a play at a local art theater. It is a murder mystery in which the chief suspect is a book! A preposterous fantasy—but if you think a book can be dangerous, well, we have one here.

The response to both play and book has been interesting. I

expected and hoped for controversy over "the violence pages" and "the finding out pages" and even "the altered states of consciousness pages." But all the scandal and notoriety has been over "the magic word pages" and "the sex pages." What I thought was comic relief in the midst of some real tension over violence and guilt became the main focal point of criticism.

The controversy over superficial things like magic words seems to be a favorite way in which The Powers That Be hamper consideration of the serious questions. Anglo-Saxon words offend some people, especially "churchy" people, more than that obscene military budget. I mean—nerve gas? What for? Intended for whom? And additional nuclear weapons, beyond the tens of thousands we have and don't know what to do with or where to store? Classes in torture, exported to places all over the world, especially in Latin America? Isn't that obscene? Shouldn't sensitive people be asking pointed questions?

Someone asked John Calvin about the origin and logic of his teachings concerning the Will of God. A similar scene arises whenever an aware child asks, "Who made God?" Calvin responded, "That's an impudent question," and of course he didn't answer it, because he couldn't.

The same attitude is all-pervasive in our time, in these last days of the American Empire. There is more secrecy than ever, in spite of protestations to the contrary. Every government agency resorts to secrecy. The enemy from whom these millions of secrets must be kept is the sovereign people.

The Vatican operates in secrecy. The refusal of John Paul II to investigate the murder of John I—his immediate predecessor who lived/served just thirty-three days as Pope—implicates him in the conspiracy, at least after the fact if not before.

The Presbyterian Church used to conduct some of its business at the presbytery level "in executive session," meaning in secret. No good ever came of any use of that practice that I knew of while

I was involved. I came to believe that it would have been better, in every case, to announce from the housetops whatever it was that someone wanted kept secret.

"There shall be no illegal questions." I believe it now more than ever. My work, my daily work, consists of opening up closed doors, uncovering what is hidden, making conscious what is unconscious, and then telling it. "There shall be nothing secret that shall not be made known." You can just count on it.

People call me too blunt, too frank, too clear, too candid, too honest, too simple. Maybe so. I have found that without secrets there is no need to hide. If you tell the truth, you don't have to remember the previous web of lies, the daisy chain of falsehoods—you can just reiterate the truth. At its root, life is simple. All the complications are excuses, extenuating circumstances, rationalizations, explanations, and appeals for special treatment.

I recall an incident at the time I was leaving the church. My friend and first tutor in Spanish had come all the way from Spain to be on the faculty of that last summer camp I was to direct. By then I knew I was leaving. He and I debated, not always patiently, my course of action. My friend's wife watched us, and then indicated that she thought I was doing the right thing. He was shocked. *"¡Su vida! ¡Su futuro!"* (His life! His future!) my friend exclaimed.

"No, Emilio. Hay que ser sencillo." It doesn't translate very well into English. *"Sencillo"* means uncomplicated, clear, true, basic. "It is necessary to be simple." I understood it, and have heard those words guiding me ever since. *"Hay que ser sencillo."*

Years later, when a local editor rejected a story of mine as "too simple," I took it as a compliment and felt sorry for his complicated life and mind, and for his readers. I haven't shown him anything since.

33. MISANTHROPY

A dear friend of mine, a man now more than eighty years old, has come to the conviction that the human species is doomed. He mocks the shortness of our dominance on earth when compared to the millions of years the dinosaurs ruled. He has listed eighteen serious problems confronting humanity, including overpopulation, love of fighting and destroying, large scale worldwide militarization, malnutrition, government by liars, poisoned and depleted soil, nuclear waste, poisoned fresh water, poisoned oceans, global warming, dislike of historical truth, preference for myths/religion, increased nationalism and ethnocentrism, the arming with government power of various kinds of fanatical fundamentalism, and so forth.

His list is impressive, and his arguments irresistible, when looked at from a purely logical point of view. The last item on his list is the fact that no government is seriously trying to do anything about any of the previous items on the list. But lately Tom has begun to do more than think logically. He is saying that humanity is despicable, deserves to be extincted, and when we are all gone the world will be better off. He has become a classic card-carrying misanthrope, a hater of mankind.

Gulliver's Travels has long been at the absolute top of my list of Great Books. In 1726 Jonathan Swift analyzed correctly some remarkably modern phenomena: tyrants, bureaucrats, militarists, lawyers, health care specialists and research scientists. Swift is described by most literary critics as a misanthrope, but I believe the charge is unfounded.

Swift's character, Gulliver, becomes a misanthrope at the end of Book IV. He has come to hate his wife, simply because she is human, and prefers spending his time in the stable with the horses. The king of Brobdignag in Book II has some devastating things to say about Gulliver's species, most notably, "I cannot but conclude [from what Gulliver has told him directly] the bulk of your natives to be the most pernicious race of little odious vermin that nature ever suffered to crawl upon the surface of the earth."

But that doesn't make Swift the author a misanthrope. I believe the exact opposite case could be made. Much of Swift's indignation has in it a frustrated *love* of humanity and a profound disappointment that we never seem to do better.

I don't see any love of humanity left in my friend. When he states how "humans love to kill," he glares and tightens his mouth, as if *he* could kill. He has quite a bit of self-hate in him, and from time to time he turns on me, even though he has often called me the best friend he has in the world. What disgusts him about me is that I have not yet quite fully given up on humanity. I keep getting involved in some of those causes that are designed to prevent or delay the extinction of our species.

For example, a group of us are trying to hinder the U.S. government's production of additional nuclear weapons and the strewing of the resulting nuclear waste all over the nation and the world. The Dutch boy with his finger in the dike could hold back the ocean, but this attempt on the part of a few private citizens to take on the Department of Defense, so-called, and the Department of Energy, so-called, really is ridiculous. Tom isn't the only one who tells me so.

The inhabitants of this city and this state will be among the first to be extinct—they're setting up several new Chernobles here, and lying, lying, lying about it. Most of my fellow citizens want to believe the DOE, and those who know we dare not have fallen into such despair as to wonder if we might as well go on with our paltry lives with little or no regard for future generations. Tom himself says, "What is left to do, except hope for a few more years in moderate comfort?"

There's that word "comfort" again. I hear echoes of thirty years ago. "Don't bring us truth! We want comfort!" So, it's word-study time again. Comfort means "with strength." What? To lie around fed and at ease, while liars lie and radiation destroys the biosphere itself? No, "with strength" to outlast them, to endure, to do something, to tell the world, at least.

I guess I believe in something that Tom doesn't. I wonder what it is. Not "God." I do not believe that the Christian war god exists. If he does, I declare again, here and now, that I despise him. I dedicate myself to *his* extinction. I dedicate myself to oppose everything he stands for, including all his pretending to be loving when he isn't. He is an idol. He is a reflection of those who invented him and those who still worship him. He is a projection onto the Cosmos of the essential meanness of the likes of Gerald Falwell, Patrick Robertson, Patrick Buchanan and Pope John Paul II. But above and beyond that nasty little idol is something more. Truth. Reality. Something in the name of which I can see and disapprove of the nastiness in humans. I find my loyalty soaring above the humans.

I have another friend and fellow protestor, who also can give indications of misanthropy. We were protesting the plan to do away with environmental protection laws and the rights of organized labor in the name of international trade. He told me, "It'll collapse, Harry. It'll collapse of its own weight, its own inner rot—whether we protest or not." He was almost gloating.

What will collapse? This system we have made—this government, these corporations, this arrangement of stocks, insurance, credit, concentrated capital, profit—it is collapsing and will come to a conclusion, whether we protest or not. They always do, these systems we build. "Oh where are kings and empires now, of old that went and came?"

I take comfort from geology. Whatever we're fretting about, a hundred years from now it won't matter. A hundred million years from now it really won't matter. Our species, and all our empires and our art and our philosophy, will all be gone.

I take comfort from astronomy. It takes four years for the light from the Alpha Centauri star system, the nearest one to ours, to get here. I'm glad that our MRV-bombs and B-2 stealth bombers and biological warfare substances will never reach them. Over there they are safe from us. What happened to the Arawaks and the Mohicans and the Susquehannocks will not happen to them. And if our planet becomes like the moon because of our foolishness and our meanness, maybe it's just as well. And if it doesn't, and new unimaginable life forms evolve here after we've gone and our garbage has finally dissipated after ten thousand generations—250,000 years, not long really—then I'll be pleased.

Sometimes I think my disgust with humanity is an exaggerated response to my great disappointment with the United States of America. "The dream dies hard" describes my political awakening over decades—my growing awareness that far from being the best country on earth, ours has come to be one of the worst. This country is no different from all the others on the long list of too-large concentrations of power. Power has been and is being misused, *as always*. "Power corrupts and absolute power corrupts absolutely."

As a nation we pretend to believe in equality, in universal human dignity, in peace and prosperity, but our nation's budget indicates that we do not. We believe in power. We're not even consistent about turning power into profit. The destruction of the Sandinista revolution in Nicaragua is a case in point. It was an exercise in naked power. The intent was to increase suffering and deprivation for the sick and the hungry. Here at home one of our local senators voted for more nerve gas, and then announced that our country cannot afford to provide measles vaccine for the children. "It's a good idea," he said, "but there's no money for that."

So, I become more disgusted, more alienated, more angry, and misanthropy begins to look like not a bad idea, after all. Power corrupts, no matter how little of it a government official is allowed. "The Man without a Country" is a true short story by Edward Everett Hale that I recall from grade school days. It seemed a shameful and tragic condition then, to be a man without a country, but now it is quite appealing. I often state that I don't believe in countries. It is unwise to say it aloud while standing in customs inspection lines, I found out.

When we were traveling in the USSR and in Scandinavia, I became wistful. It must be great to be a Dane. You don't have to be ashamed of your country, your government, your history, the deeds of your forebears. You don't have to disavow loyalty, to seek always something higher and more abstract, as I find myself doing.

Having said all that, I still find myself attracted to, and even somehow attached to, the company of truth-tellers—Amos, Hosea, Jeremiah, II Isaiah, the author of the Book of Jonah, and others in other traditions, like Cassandra and Socrates. Truth-tellers are never part of the ruling group, never part of the majority. The spirit they reveal is corrupted badly, almost utterly, by institutionalization. Any kind of organization, what the ecclesiastics call "order," smothers it—bishops and popes, credentials for priests and even credentials for prophets, which is a self-contradictory notion, budgets, tithes, temples, titles—all that drowns out the spirit, which blows where it pleases and accomplishes a mysterious hidden purpose in spite of lying and murder and betrayal and excommunication in high places. Prophets don't have credentials, except this inner compulsion to say what people don't want to hear.

What was that? Am I claiming to be a prophet, another truth-teller? What arrogance! And yet, the same story insists on acting itself out in me. I'd rather shut up. I'd rather quietly cane my chairs and tend my garden. But I cannot. Something insists that I announce the truth—even in such ridiculous ways as shouting back at the television, just to prevent the lying from coming into our living room unchallenged.

So, for purposes of argument, let's say I'm a prophet. A minor prophet. Maybe like Zephaniah, really minor. How can I be a prophet, if there is no God to call me to be one and to give me a message to deliver? No "Thus saith the Lord!"

Watch that Spirit. Watch it in history. See it working in Cassandra. They said she was crazy, just because she could see clearly and had the courage to say what no one wanted to hear. The little boy who saw that the emperor was naked and simply said so —he's another one. Watch how that Spirit blows. What is it up to? It uses people, unlikely people, to carry forward something. But, *what*? Some sense of truth, some awareness of right, some ability to care. I think those able to care constitute the pool through which the Spirit moves. Who is it using now? Who can tell? Who cares?

I am in the middle of writing a novel, stalled just now because a key character has AIDS and I don't know enough personally yet about AIDS. Part of the book contains a serious consideration of the question, "What are we supposed to be doing?" Tentative answers: Be honest. Be faithful to truth. Be gentle, if possible, but not at the expense of truth. Stay clear of institutions. Do not take yourself seriously at all. See the humor in all this, the ludicrous incongruity of an uncredentialed old truth-teller trying to delay the collapse of the largest and most evil empire in the history of humanity. See to your part of the work, not the Spirit's and not other mere humans'—the results are not your concern.

No comparisons, especially to the "successful." Remember the false prophets, who thrived, and still thrive. The best poets are unpublished, or published anonymously and/or posthumously. It only happens when you aren't looking. You know what to do—go and do it. All else is stalling, including even—perhaps, probably—this enquiry.

And what is this Spirit, Harry? You snuck that in very cleverly. Now you'll say it's a metaphor, like the Muse. You like that metaphor, too. Meaning what? Metaphors referring to what?

Something. Some aspect of How It Is. Not an Entity. Not a person or a personality. Deeper than that. Bigger than that. The Whole Thing. The Ground of Everything. It impels me to say things I know are true, even though no one is listening.

Be prepared to have people call you crazy. When you call it "God," you can go get credentials—the very ones you once threw away, Harry. Without credentials you are a heretic, and without the "God," you're crazy. Schizophrenics hear voices. Paranoids feel pursued, by things like your "hound of heaven." Obsessives do things contrary to their own self-interest or survival. The world won't have to reach very far to find reasons to call you crazy.

A World For the Meek retells the Noah myth. It has turned into a kind of Rorschach test. It seems to separate the open-minded from the closed-minded. Those who like it like it very much and thank me for it. Those who don't like it make fun of it in various ways, but in so doing reveal their discomfort with openness. The story goes like this:

Our hero survives the Blast and thinks he's the last human in the world. When the dolphins find him, they think they've found a live fossil. They didn't think there were any humans left. They have history and science and philosophy and literature. It's their world now—a world for the meek. They are curious and utterly sensual. The object of the game of life for them is "to share the knowing." In the end, the dolphins are setting up a meeting between Noah and a female "land-crawler" they have found.

Tom, my misanthropic friend, sees the ending as my cop-out, allowing the humans another chance. The novel expresses my hope that human meanness and foolishness will not extinct the biosphere. It celebrates my hope, my belief, that The Whole Thing is somehow all right.

This is the comfort I have to offer. The Whole Thing is all right.

There is something misanthropic about the basic doctrine of

Christianity, at least of the preliminary doctrine of sin. Humans are flawed, it says. Calvin seemed to make out that they were wholly despicable. Some medieval Roman Catholics said the same thing, especially about women. Of course, the rest of the doctrine says that God loved humanity so much, in spite of sin, that he gave his only-begotten Son, and so forth. It's a sort of divine cure for misanthropy.

For a long time I thought my inability to believe that anymore was unusual on my part. It felt like a flaw, in the early stages, and then, later, something of an accomplishment. Recently I found this quotation in William Yalom's *Love's Executioner*: "The more one is able to tolerate the anxiety of not knowing, the less need is there for one to embrace orthodoxy. The creative members of an orthodoxy, any orthodoxy, ultimately outgrow their disciplines." That happened to me.

And now I've come to believe that no one believes it. No one. Those who profess it most and loudest believe it least. Those who have thought it through carefully and strictly, thoroughly and honestly, know that they don't really believe it. At some deep level they do believe in something, something else. Truth, let's call it. But *no one* really believes that stuff as it is stated.

The worst cynics and liars among them don't even believe in mathematics or physics. Causation—implying responsibility for one's actions—is foreign to them. They won't hear of The Undeviating Justice. They believe only in the paltry little ego with its balance sheet of "sin." What a fragile worthless thing to put one's trust in!

34. EGO AND SELF

Among all my files on Biblical studies, arranged in manila folders, one for each book of the Bible, I found a folder called *God and Green Stamps*. This was a collection of sermons of mine, arranged as a book for publication. I recall some of the rejection letters I received from publishers then, one in particular: "These should be done, but no denominational house will touch them."

I read parts of it, and became thankful that they were *not* published in 1963, or ever. If they had been, I would have had a little fame, perhaps, a little sense of success at the enterprise of ecclesiasticating, even though my sermons tended to be anti-institutional. I would have been unable to move, or would have found it much harder to move, out of the church, out of that way of thinking, and out into fresh air.

I would not be me. I would not have written *A World For the Meek*, or *This'll Kill Ya*, or *Myth and Mortality*. I am thankful, and from that I will learn to believe that the rest of what I have written and will write will be published, or not, *at the right time*.

Meanwhile, I become more aware of the rush of time. I remember old folks saying that time seems to move faster when you're older, and they weren't kidding. Now the Voice doesn't call my name—it doesn't even know my name—but it does berate me for not getting tasks accomplished. "You'll not get it done." "You're slacking." "Your efforts are insufficient." Sometimes the Voice parodies one of my most unfavorite verses: "You are an unprofitable servant. You have only done a little bit of what was your duty." When I look up the passage from which the original verse came, I see that it is a story designed to squelch incipient clerical arrogance. I recall the gross and bloody history, which indicates what little effect the story had. And when I think of that verse still troubling this infantile ex-follower, especially in his sleep, I have to yelp, "It isn't fair!"

Fair? Where'd that idea come from? Where'd I get the notion that things ought to be fair? Or that I ought to help make them more nearly fair? Whole schools of psychological therapy these days are built around the notion that one must accept the simple fact that things aren't fair, the cosmos isn't fair, the universe is indifferent

Big Questions Remain

and not fair. I still see that as a step backward into something like despair.

In my calm alert waking state I know that the Voice is ridiculous. I cannot do more than I am doing, so the pressure from within is really hostile and self-destructive. In conscious response, I find myself deliberately calming myself down, slowing myself down. Even the decision to make this enquiry is part of that effort. The attempt to market manuscripts is endless and discouraging, and consumes and wastes large amounts of energy and time. I find that actual success in that enterprise comes only in unexpected and unimagined ways anyway, so I have decided to cool the frantic, fruitless effort. This enquiry could turn into one more manuscript that the Voice will tell me I must break my tail trying to market. But my intent is not that at all. Instead, I'm trying to find out what I believe.

I have found that there is a source of energy that I can tap into by ceasing the frantic effort. "Be still and know that I am God." There's a voice, someone's voice, recorded in the Book of Psalms. Not that Voice that frightens and berates. It feels like the one single subconscious Mind-Will, seeking to express itself through me. It is in no hurry. It is never thwarted, or disappointed. It has forever.

That damned Voice of *mine* is my ego. As old as my infancy and *still* infantile, my ego says, "You gotta do this, you haven't yet done that. What about this other thing? Time is running out! Get to work! No rest for the wicked. Work, for the night is coming." It's all ego, sometimes trying to pacify the superego probably, but all ego, wanting credit, wanting to be paid, wanting to be recognized.

When I write this stuff, and stumble on insights like that, it is pure pleasure. The ability to meditate not moving for hours like a yogi is not my style. But a pen and a notebook—that's my Zen. I learn things. I calm my soul. I quiet my ego. Get thee hence, you puny comical little troubler.

The careers of Sigmund Freud and Karl Gustav Jung can be

taken as metaphors for the two halves of a human life. Freud deals with the first half, when the task is to build an ego that can withstand the pressures of being a live individual in the midst of a human society. You have to become somebody. Jung then gives attention to the second-half task, which is to give up ego, to transcend ego, and finally to be reabsorbed into the overarching Self of the World.

The fact that Dylan Thomas could write, "Do Not Go Gentle into that Good Night," indicates that it is not enough to create beauty, to be an artist who creates works that impose a human meaning on the cosmos. There is something else that must be done, something on the inside.

It must begin with introspection, without much public announcement of what is being discovered, especially in the early stages. Some introspection is little more than ego-justification. But in order to get ready to die gracefully, gently, one will have to find out what the ego, one's own little comical puffed-up ego, was invented for. Then one will have to do whatever that is, or give it the absolutely best try possible. Then one can place ego back into its cosmic context, transfer loyalty back to the Self of the World and away from the perishable ego. It is a lifelong task.

Raging against the fact that individual organisms die is a sign of clinging to ego, and may indicate that the second-stage task has not been completed, or perhaps not yet undertaken at all. One has trouble dying, when one has not yet lived. And if that person moves on into the collapse-of-the-vehicle stage, if body or brain give out—especially brain—the result for many persons is tragic.

The first-half task, for me, was hindered and delayed by the expectations laid on me by my parents. The first half of my life consisted of gradually throwing them off. My non-abrupt way of dealing with them led me into all those years spent trying to be a professional clergyman. Those expectations were so utterly ridiculous that the telling of them now comes across as hilarious.

Big Questions Remain 213

I feel like an idiot for having let them have any influence on me at all.

When I announced that I was not going to medical school but to seminary instead, my father said to me, "And I thought you were the one who would discover the cure for cancer, which killed my mother." It did no good for me to explain how research was done, that no one person was going to discover the cure for cancer, that cancer was at least partly a metaphor for *inner* things anyway. He was simply grossly disappointed and managed to make me feel bad for disappointing him.

When I announced that I was leaving the church, leaving the position of clergyman, which felt to me like the local operator of a huge international psychological racket, my father said to me, "And I thought you were the one who would reform the church, like Martin Luther." It did no good for me to explain how Luther did not reform the church, but simply divided it, that no one person was ever going to reform that bloody institution. I used the word "bloody" partly literally and partly as one of my mother's Scottish cuss words.

When I wrote letters telling of some of my feelings of success as a teacher of young boys, my father wrote back that I should go into politics and become Senator from New Mexico and lead the struggle to end the Vietnam War. By that time I was on my own enough, at last, to laugh that one off and not reply at all.

I did have a great deal of resentment about expectations, and they contributed to the distance during those ten years I stayed away. I wrote letters, but they weren't all kind and deferent, and some were no doubt no fun to read. "The parent-child relationship is hereby ended, for lack of a child." Knowing that I was a gross disappointment to them—a kind of outcast, the black sheep in the family—contributed to the distance and sense of wariness.

When my parents died, the last pressure of the ridiculous expectations went away. Thank the Great Spirit, I do not, after all, have to be a combination of Louis Pasteur, Martin Luther and Mahatma Gandhi in order to be an all-right human being.

What kind of infantilism was it, my letting all that be anything but a joke? There are those who simply do what they want to do. I have watched them and envied them. How do they do it? It's a little hard to describe—the words take away the wonder—they simply do not do what they do not want to do. What a mystery! I have spent hours, afternoons, days, months, years, doing what I did not want to do.

Way back in high school, I wrestled with what I thought was the Big Question, "What does God want me to do with my life?" What *I* wanted to do with my life never entered into it.

When I began studying mythology, to put myself back together after leaving the womb of Holy Mother Church, I discovered that the First Great Question was, "What do you want?" The first step in becoming an alchemist, a Wielder of Power, is, "What do you want?" You're not going to get power if you don't know yet what you want it for.

"What do you want, Harry?" The question felt new and strange, and dangerous. Looking back across vast areas of my life, I could see that the question had never been allowed to surface. But it had been at work beneath the surface. I wanted to marry. I wanted to study mythology, not biochemistry. I wanted to divorce and marry someone else. And I did all three of those things, and they determined the direction of my life. The expectations of my father were simply the obstructions I had to work against.

So, I'm studying alchemy, and the First Great Question is out in the open: "What do you want?" It turns out there's a thing in alchemy that brings it all full circle. If you want and use your power for self-aggrandizing, personal, unworthy aims, like money and influence and fame, that's *black* magic, and in the end you will be destroyed.

No, "what you want" is It—whatever you want to call it, I find the term God too badly contaminated—It, the Cosmos, The Whole Thing—what you want is It expressing itself as Desire *through you.* You are the vehicle It uses, the Chariot which It drives and rides. So, after all, it's not a case of getting free of "external forces." I, and all of us, are enmeshed in them, no matter what. Even the most self-centered have to obey the law of gravity, and their blood must circulate. They aren't quite as "free" as they look. In my case, I felt an exhilarating sense of liberation from paltry little meaningless expectations imposed in infancy, wrongly and unfairly. And I find I have had some rather remarkable practice at being Someone Else's vehicle.

This has become one of the basic things that I have come to believe. Each of us must become self-aware enough to be able to answer that first great question, "What do you want?" This is not in order to enhance "selfishness"—a word that has been used for ages to keep individuals in line. "Don't be so selfish!" "You're being very selfish!" Usually it means, "You're not doing what I want!" The poor children, then adolescents, then adults who let this govern their lives never develop a Self.

Each of us needs to grow a Self, to become Somebody—not an appendage of someone else. We need love and a safe place and encouragement, but we do *not* need to be the instruments by which other persons try to express their selfhood. Each tub must stand on its own bottom. Then, when we have a Self—when we are somebody, and we have something to give, to contribute, to share—then those of us who have this strange curiosity about Cosmic Purpose can offer to the One-going Process something that is free and alive, rather than a dead appendage of something else.

I tried giving what I didn't have. I tried pretending to be what I wasn't. When I began to grow a Self, many called the things I began to do selfish. It seems to me now that it had to be done, and would have been less painful all around if it had been done sooner, without the long detour through imagined, phony self-*less*-ness.

True selflessness comes at the end of the life process.

The essential trick, which I learned not from Christianity but from the Orient and the Tarot, is to transfer loyalty from ego to Self. What am I? If I am ego, it is doom for sure. Ego is so picayune, so mean at heart, so frail, so in error, so temporary, so undependable. But to the extent that I am Self—It, the Self of the World, the One Mind-Will that expresses itself in all these body-ego vehicles—to that extent, I am understanding, patient, invincible. It's a game, an exercise. It is pretending to be Me, the ego, but I'm onto the trick now. I know better in my deepest gut awareness, I can even laugh about it. I can watch the decline and fall of empires, and maybe also my favorite species, with a kind of wry detachment.

The Self business is like learning to ride a bicycle. I've had it rolling a little, but it's still shaky and I still fall a lot. But it's getting better, and I'll soon get the hang of it. Just a few more incarnations, maybe.

Someone told Thomas Carlyle that Lady Whatsername had decided to accept the Universe. "By God, she'd better!" he retorted.

John Calvin asked his students and readers, "Are you willing to be damned to the glory of God?" It's an ego question, surely. God—for Calvin, the Sovereign Almighty Creator and Ruler of the Universe—demands your utter loyalty and worship. His Will is irresistible. Calvin intended that his readers would reply instantly, "Yes! We are ready and willing to be damned to the eternal glory of God! We are so indebted to God for his grace in creating us, and then redeeming us through Christ—yes! We are ready, ready and willing!"

Of course, it's a trick question. When the candidate for ordination was asked that same question by the Chairman of the Committee on Examinations on the floor of presbytery, he replied, "Not only that, Good Sir. I'm willing that this entire presbytery be damned to the glory of God!" This was in the old days; they did not ordain him, due to his excessive public levity.

It's a trick question. Persons who are willing to be damned, that is, to be cast out forever beyond the reach of God's Love, are not loving God. Persons who can imagine living without God are not loving God.

The trick answer is that shift from ego to Self. An ego that is willing to be destroyed is on the right track. It will be destroyed! And then the Self, which is left after the ego is damned and gone, will be reabsorbed into what it was all along, the One Self of the World.

I suspect that Calvin wouldn't like my shifting the ground here, but he set it up with his trick question. Are you willing—am I willing?—to be the Self that rides a vehicle, rather than the vehicle that is ridden?

I'd better be!

35. CONCLUSION

The best symbol for my own myth, what's left of my "belief system," is the numeral One. I am a Monist. There is One. It is all one. What There Is is an organic mechanism, which is *not* a contradiction in terms! It is alive, conscious, totally interconnected, irresistible, whole, total, integrated, expressive, beautiful, just, perfect.

The following statements constitute "What I Know for Sure," tested by personal direct experience, dependable enough to stake my life on:

The unexamined life is not worth living.

Many of my fellow humans live lives of quiet desperation.

Self-deception is an ever-lurking danger.

Humans, including me, often prefer to be excused from responsibility.

Life is more lively when I take responsibility and act.

Change is not my enemy.
Good things happen mostly when I'm not looking.
The love and loyalty of a good mate are worth more than success or reputation.
A good sound failure does wonders in opening up new opportunities for growth.
Persons, including me, do not learn much by being told.
Liars destroy language itself.
It is easier to give than to receive.
The spirit is willing, but the flesh is busy.
Desire will not be permanently thwarted.
Arriving home is the best part of traveling.
A person cannot be faulted for beginning where he did.
The best preparation for Death is to pack in a lot of living.
The Whole Thing is all right.
I will discover additional truths as I go along.

❖ ❖ ❖

PART IV

◆

AFTERWORDS

36. EDITOR'S INTERLUDE

Writers like Harry do not leave themselves anything to hide behind. Over and over he demanded absolute honesty—"The truth and nothing but the truth"—as best he could determine it. His truth, his Self, his ego, his attitudes were subjected to repeated scrutiny and refinement. His scriptomania constituted a "Report to Base" (the title of one of his many short stories)—an ongoing check-in with the collective consciousness he called The Cosmos, and those friends, colleagues and readers who travel the same path of enquiry. And so I feel it my duty to report on the conclusion of Harry's life study, his study of life and his life.

It was a good thing that he heeded his own advice and went about his work as he did. He didn't have nearly as many years ahead of him as he must have imagined when he wrote this "philosophical memoir" at the age of 62. Fifteen years was all. They flew by. They were filled with wonderful adventures for Harry and Adela, accomplishments and greater recognition—but never enough for Harry—"precious little," he would say. The "father" thing never fully went away. He really did crave validation from The Powers That Be, at least in the publishing world, preferably in the form of cash. The basement, the office, the shed—make that two sheds—were full of books. The publishing business was literally weighing him down, and the manuscripts were piling up.

Things got more difficult personally as well. The last few years found him doing a lot of stuff he didn't want to do, as happens when one ages and the body needs more maintenance, and family and friends need more help, too. But he never stopped doing his thing, or delighting in the "good stuff"— friends, love, nature, art, music, work. With his spiral notebook and a pen near at hand, Harry could get through all difficulties by stepping outside of himself to observe, contemplate and articulate the puzzle of being alive, miserable, and conscious of it. From a more objective vantage, it was even possible to laugh.

While going through this manuscript, I kept thinking, "This is exactly what he did. He laid out his task for himself and he did it." He got over ego quite a lot. He stuck to his principles. He kept writing. He kept speaking out. He even learned to go to meetings, where he found community with the local Friendly Philosophers group, and, through them, the Humanist Society of New Mexico. He was utterly devoted to Adela, incredibly patient with me. Too patient, it turned out; we had no idea how little time was left.

He faced death bravely, lucidly. He took complete responsibility and control from the moment he was diagnosed with and began being treated for cancer, which proved to be virulent, until the day he accepted that it could not be arrested with radiation therapy. He called off the treatment in order to resume holding court for the stream of visitors who came to his bedside day and night, sometimes crowding in and making the whole scene seem like a party. Harry delighted in the outpouring of love, wouldn't abide pity, converted our sadness into a kind of hilarity, and kept asking, remarking, shaking his head at the puzzling mystery, the gross indelicacy, the utter irony of the whole dying process.

When Harry "threw in the towel" he did so irrevocably. He decided to decline food, and feedings once the time came when he couldn't eat on his own. He gave up carrying a cellphone in the pocket of his flannel shirt. Up until then, it was still possible to dial a number and have him pick up: "Harry Willson speaking." He had found himself and his own good strong voice.

Let it be recorded that Harry Willson, at the end of his enquiry *as* Harry Willson, faced death without fear, though not without some indignation at its coming so soon. He was still full of wonder at the beauty of life and not eager to give it up. His sole worry was for Adela, and when he had confided his distress at no longer being able to care for her to enough of us, enough times, he finally laid down that last burden and let the time remaining be what it was for the two of them—decrepit, disrupted, but together—with half of Albuquerque parading through.

I can't speak for Harry's eternal soul, or his next incarnation, or say if the Harry generated by my dreams is anything more than memory and longing. He made a skeptic of me, more of one, so there is no ghost of Harry to answer to. I wonder—fifteen years later, would he have expunged all references to "spirit" from his manuscript, had he been editing it himself? He came to dislike the word "spiritual" almost as much as he disliked the word "God." Was that because he no longer believed in spirit, or because he had refined his concept of spirit such that glib avowals of "spirituality" offended him?

There is no disputing that the totality of Harry's writings amounts to a physical and conceptual manifestation of his spirit that did not go "Blotto" when the vehicle that was Harry Willson blipped off our radar. That was the whole point of his insisting on so much honesty, so much openness, and putting so much of himself into every effort. Harry Willson happened. He recorded what was happening to him right up to the end. Following are Harry's last two monthly web site columns, written in January and February 2010.

37. CARE

The word "care" has been batted around a great deal lately. Let me take part in the action.

For two weeks now I have been in a rehabilitation facility, following serious surgery on my spine. The therapists who work here are not kidding around. They want me and all their patients to improve enough to get out of here. They work very hard. They are often out of breath and must stop for air. They make us work hard too, one therapist after another. It really is exhausting!

But I notice it is all care, i.e., caring. Never a harsh word, always an encouraging word. The old word that I come up with to describe what they do is "love."

Jay E. was here yesterday. At one point I exclaimed, "It's amazing! You can make your living loving people!" Jay jumped up and made a placard saying just that, which he then hung on the wall.

The theme in my mind is "care." Care is caring. I am watching so much of it, I am overwhelmed. Not "coverage." That's a different topic. We all talk of health care. Some talk of health coverage. But that's not what I'm looking at. Care is caring. Coverage is legalese, and look out!

I'm not sure this even is a rant. "Rant" implies a degree of indignation, and what I'm referring to now is a series of experiences which leaves me in a kind of meltdown. Absorb the love. Return it. Not much in the way of indignation.

This experience makes a body thoughtful. It "concentrates the mind." I think of my whole life, and it occurs to me that for a period I made my living loving people. The ten years that I taught school are what I'm thinking of. The students came first with me, and everybody knew it, and at times it caused trouble, what with

Afterwords 225

institutional rules and traditions and reputations and all that. But the students knew.

I'm wondering what a country more concerned about care than coverage would look like.

38. THOUGHTS WHILE PLAYING THE PIANO

I look at my audience and wonder what they're thinking. Why would a man in a plastic brace over his chest and abdomen (I call it "the turtle shell"), sitting in a partially dismantled wheelchair, want to try to entertain similarly handicapped persons by playing the big black grand piano in the dining room of the Canyon Rehabilitation Center? I wonder myself. I think it does me good—I'm not sure it helps them much.

At home I play a little $400 keyboard. All I have to do to get sound out of it is touch the keys. The grand piano is different and I have to strike the keys with enough force to carry through a long and complicated series of connections. But I'm doing it, or trying to. The errors don't improve the finished concert project, but the effort is worth it nevertheless.

I am not a very good pianist. Why me? How did this happen? There was a sign on the impressive grand piano in the corner of the dining room: "Do not play the piano." My son Andy asked the woman from administration, "What does this sign mean?" She said, "Oh, that's for people who can't play the piano." Andy said, "My Dad can play the piano." Next thing I know, I'm playing for the dining room audience, before breakfast and before lunch.

Now I have a theme song. It is "Boogie Woogie 1942." I inflict on this strange audience all the stuff I've been trying to memorize, all the way from "Arkansas Traveler" to "Elmer's Tune" and "Why Don't You Do Right? " Already people are bringing me stuff to play. I read music fairly well, so I give it a try, slowly at first, but it picks up with repetition. Things like "Go Down, Moses" and "Seeing Nellie Home."

I look again at the audience. The majority are incapable of any type of participation or response. A few nod their heads in correct time with the music. Some in the audience really get into the rhythm by moving loose body parts. My mistakes throw them off, but that doesn't seem to bother them much.

There is a class of people, I suppose, who would find all of this dreadful. But not everyone does—I have received signals from handicapped (former) musicians. And people who care about me are glad that I have this opportunity. And people who care for individuals in the audience thank me for the effort.

It still seems that this whole business has more to do with me than anyone else. Writing is very different under the current circumstances. Mounting that required effort tells you more about me than it tells me about you.

What a strange thought, come to me while playing the piano in a strange set of circumstances!

Harry Willson
1932–2010

Harry Willson was born in Montoursville, Pennsylvania. He received his undergraduate degree in chemistry and math at Lafayette College in Easton, Pennsylvania, and a Master of Divinity in ancient Middle-Eastern language and literature at Princeton Theological Seminary. He became bilingual through one year of Spanish studies at the University of Madrid, and holds the *Diploma de Español como Lengua Extranjera* from the University of Salamanca, Spain. Later he studied Spanish, literature, philosophy, mythology, and theater arts at the University of New Mexico. He served as student pastor at the Presbyterian Church, Hamburg, New Jersey, for four years while in seminary. In 1958, Harry moved his family to New Mexico, where he served as bilingual missionary pastor in Bernalillo, Alameda, and Placitas for eight years. He served as Permanent Clerk of the Presbytery of Rio Grande, Chairman of Enlistments and Candidates, Chairman of the Commission on Race, and Moderator of the Presbytery.

In 1965, Harry answered Dr. Martin Luther King Jr.'s call for clergy to go to Selma, Alabama to assist in voter registration and demonstrations against police brutality. He participated in the successful march from Selma to Montgomery on March 25, where he personally witnessed Dr. King deliver his "How Long, Not Long" speech. Not long after that, in 1966, Harry left the church "in sorrow and anger" over its failure to take a stand against the Vietnam War. He spent the summer of 1967 on the staff of the Southern Christian Leadership Conference in Atlanta, assigned as their representative to the Atlanta Alliance for Peace.

After quitting the clergy, Harry taught for ten years, first at the Albuquerque Academy and then at Sandia Preparatory School, after which he retired from teaching to devote himself to his writing. His fiction and nonfiction attracted a diverse and enthusiastic audience. From 1996 to 2010, he wrote a "Rant of the Month" column for the Amador Publishers web site, totaling more than 150 essays. He was also published in a variety of local and national periodicals, and several of his one-act plays were produced. Readers frequently corresponded with Harry to let him know how they were personally touched by his writing; some claimed he had changed their lives.

About the Editor
Zelda Leah Gatuskin

Zelda Leah Gatuskin is a native of Wilmington, Delaware, and graduate of Emerson College in Boston. She moved to Albuquerque, New Mexico in 1983, and opened her creative arts and design business, "Studio Z," in 1988. Her visual artwork has been shown in local venues and published as cover and interior book illustration.

In 1989, Harry Willson of Amador Publishers took Zelda under wing and launched her literary career with the publication of her first novel, *The Time Dancer*. Several more books followed: *Ancestral Notes*, *Castle Lark*, *Time and Temperature*, and *Zelda's Cosmic Coloring Book*.

Zelda participated in a design and editorial capacity on other Amador book projects, including the *Christmas Blues* anthology, *Amerika? America!* by Eva and Manfred Krutein, *Undercurrents* by Adela Amador, and *Myth and Mortality*, the second volume in Harry Willson's humanist trilogy.

Zelda's recent publications are a collection of poetry, *But Who's Counting?*, which was a 2010 New Mexico Book Awards winner, and a novel, *Where the Sky Used to Be*, published in 2011. She has been recognized by the NMPW (New Mexico Press Women) for her monthly column in the Humanist Society of New Mexico Newsletter while serving as the organization's president.

In 2006, Zelda joined Harry and Adela as co-owner and managing editor of the press. In 2010 she succeeded Harry as editor-in-chief.

Harry Willson's Humanist Trilogy

FREEDOM FROM GOD: RESTORING THE SENSE OF WONDER (2001) is a study in candor, a philosophical broadside of profound importance, a guide to personal liberation, an invitation to wonder.

Former Pastor Willson has written an engaging and unusual account of his own release from the traps of false ideas about God and the self. His theology amounts to no less than a revival of a kind of monism, the assertion that all reality, the whole universe, is one substance. His journey will seem familiar to many agnostics and independent minds, but his account is told with zest and is supported by experience and deep feeling. Highly recommended.
—LIBRARY JOURNAL

In MYTH AND MORTALITY: TESTING THE STORIES (2007), Harry Willson works through thirty-two different beliefs or metaphors dealing with death, and gives frank evaluations of how helpful they may be. While the author challenges each reader to be ready for his or her own departure, his message is life-affirming: "Share what you know. Share what you are. Who says you're finished? Don't quit ahead of time..."

Published posthumously, FROM FEAR TO LOVE: MY JOURNEY BEYOND CHRISTIANITY was in fact the first work of the "enquiry" the author began at the age of 62. These three volumes by Harry Willson, former clergyman and committed writer-teacher-activist, offer an informed, irreverent voice of reason in a world gone mad on dogma, hype, guilt trips and power trips. Above all, Harry's commitment to personal and mutual liberation shines through.

www.amadorbooks.com

www.ingramcontent.com/pod-product-compliance
Lightning Source LLC
Chambersburg PA
CBHW071658090426
42738CB00009B/1580